ISSUES THAT CONCERN YOU

Homeschooling

Heidi Watkins, *Book Editor*

GREENHAVEN PRESS
A part of Gale, Cengage Learning

Detroit • New York • San Francisco • New Haven, Conn • Waterville, Maine • London

Elizabeth Des Chenes, *Director, Publishing Solutions*

For more information, contact:
Greenhaven Press
27500 Drake Rd.
Farmington Hills, MI 48331-3535
Or you can visit our Internet site at gale.cengage.com

For product information and technology assistance, contact us at

Gale Customer Support, 1-800-877-4253
For permission to use material from this text or product, submit all requests online at www.cengage.com/permissions

Further permissions questions can be e-mailed to permissionrequest@cengage.com

Articles in Greenhaven Press anthologies are often edited for length to meet page requirements. In addition, original titles of these works are changed to clearly present the main thesis and to explicitly indicate the author's opinion. Every effort is made to ensure that Greenhaven Press accurately reflects the original intent of the authors. Every effort has been made to trace the owners of copyrighted material.

Cover image © wavebreakmedia/Shutterstock.com.

LIBRARY OF CONGRESS CATALOGING-IN-PUBLICATION DATA

Homeschooling / Heidi Watkins, book editor.
   pages cm. -- (Issues that concern you)
 Includes bibliographical references and index.
 ISBN 978-0-7377-6296-9 (hardcover)
 1. Home schooling--Juvenile literature. I. Watkins, Heidi.
 LC40.H47 2013
 371.04'2--dc23
                                   2013003532

Printed in the United States of America
1 2 3 4 5 6 7 17 16 15 14 13

CONTENTS

Fearing imprisonment, a German couple with their five children flee to the United States where they will be safe. Eventually, a US judge grants them asylum. Their crime under German law was homeschooling. The year asylum was granted was 2010.

Homeschooling is completely illegal in Germany and many other countries, including Sweden, Greece, and Brazil. The majority of countries that do permit homeschooling do so with restrictions. For instance, in Iceland parents must hold a teaching certificate, and in Poland children are supervised by local school officials and must pass examinations every year.

In the United States parents in all fifty states do have the right to homeschool their children. Homeschooling laws vary by state, but most states have few or no restrictions. Eleven states have no requirements at all; parents do not even need to notify anyone that they are homeschooling. In about fifteen states parents must only send a letter of notification to the state. In about twenty-one states only annual standardized testing or evaluation of progress by a professional is required. Only six states highly regulate homeschooling with requirements such as curriculum approval, teacher certification, or home visits.

As this makes clear, both worldwide and in the United States, homeschooling laws vary tremendously. For governing bodies, the issue is whether homeschooling, if allowed, should be completely unregulated, somewhat regulated, or highly regulated. For homeschooling advocates, the core issue is parental rights versus government control. In the United States it is safe to say that parental rights is the rule, which is why, even though many states have some regulations, homeschooling is indeed legal.

The parental right to choose homeschooling is not without problems and opposition, however. In certain isolated but alarming cases, criminals have taken advantage of states' minimally regulated homeschooling environments to commit or cover up horrific crimes, including kidnapping and murder. Such cases have some experts calling for change.

As reported on the CBS *Evening News* in 2009, A ten-year-old boy was murdered and buried by his parents at their home. Because the parents claimed to be homeschooling, more than a year went by before anyone noticed that he was even missing. This was in Iowa, a state that moderately regulates homeschooling, requiring notification and annual test scores or evaluation.

Shawn Hornbeck, at the age of twelve, was kidnapped in rural Missouri in October 2002. After 1,558 days he was found in his kidnapper's motel room with another boy who had more recently disappeared. During the more than four years that Hornbeck was missing he was repeatedly tortured and raped. In a 2008 interview with *People* magazine, Hornbeck stated that what happened to him would "send psychiatrists insane." In part Hornbeck's kidnapper got away with it because, posing as Hornbeck's father and living in a state with unregulated homeschooling, he claimed that he was homeschooling.

As reported in the *New York Times* in January 2008, Banita Jacks murdered her four daughters, aged five to seventeen, in Washington, D.C., during the summer of 2007. The murders went undetected until January 2008, when federal marshals came to serve eviction papers and found the girls' decomposing bodies still laid out in the home. In March 2007 Jacks had been allowed to withdraw her daughters from public school because homeschooling is completely unregulated in the District of Columbia. In this case, the social services system had been involved and had failed, but critics of unregulated homeschooling assert that, had the girls continued in school while their mother's mental health was spiraling downhill, their neglect or absence could have been noticed or they could have been able to safely ask for help.

To be clear, these are not cases of homeschooling parents who are killing their children or hiding kidnapped children. Rather, they are criminals claiming to be homeschooling to avoid justice. These anecdotes do not indicate that homeschooling causes murder and kidnapping; however, the cloak of homeschooling did work for these parents and this kidnapper for a time. In each

Parents' right to homeschool their children varies from state to state, but most states have few or no restrictions regarding it.

of these cases children went missing for months or even years before they were discovered, and the children did not have the opportunity to be in school where someone could have noticed that they were in danger.

The role of parental rights is just one of the issues related to homeschooling today. Authors in this anthology examine homeschooling from a variety of angles: analyzing trends, assessing homeschooling's educational effectiveness, and debating the virtues of evangelical Christian homeschoolers, feminist homeschoolers, and the like. In addition, the volume contains several appendixes to help the reader understand and explore the topic, including a thorough bibliography and a list of organizations to contact for further information. The appendix titled "What You Should Know About Homeschooling" offers facts and statistics. The appendix "What You Should Do About Homeschooling" offers tips for young people who want to take action. With all these features, *Issues That Concern You: Homeschooling* provides a thorough resource for everyone interested in this timely issue.

ONE

Homeschooling Is a Growing Trend and Evolving Practice

Danielle Geary

> Homeschooling is a growing movement. The number of reported homeschoolers nearly tripled from 1991 to 1999, increasing from 300,000 to 805,000. Current estimates vary widely but range from 1.2 to 2 million students. Danielle Geary, a modern-language professor at the Georgia Institute of Technology (Georgia Tech) with an interest in instructional technology, examines this trend in the following viewpoint. Geary addresses technical advances that will influence homeschooling, controversies surrounding the practice, homeschooling's implications, and how homeschooled students adjust to college and university life.

In the United States, every child has the right to an education and is required by law to attend school. The government provides an enormous number of public schools throughout the country, free of charge, in order to ensure education for all, yet there are families who choose to homeschool their children instead. [Social science researcher P.] Hill explains that "homeschooling is not a new phenomenon. In colonial days families, including wealthy ones, educated their children at home, combining the efforts of parents, tutors, and older children." He goes on to men-

Danielle Geary, "Trend and Data Analysis of Homeschooling," *Academic Leadership Live*, vol. 9, no. 4, Fall 2011. Copyright © 2011 by Academic Leadership Live. All rights reserved. Reproduced by permission.

tion how colonial rural one-room schoolhouses provided a place for the children of several families to study together under the direction of a teacher who implemented their personal program of instruction.

Modern day homeschooling began in the 1970s by two main groups of people: the intensely religious and those of an exceptionally high academic philosophy. In the 1970s and 1980s, states treated homeschooling as a type of truancy, claiming that children, by law, must be in school. Initially, relations between homeschooling advocates and school authorities were very strained and often hostile. During the 1980s, advocates of home-based education came together as allies to legalize homeschooling at the state level. During the 1990s, as a result of the legalization of home-based education and the widespread use of the internet, homeschooling began to grow and became a viable option for more families. These families represent a demographically diverse group of people; from Christians to atheists, libertarians to liberals, low-income families to high-income families, blacks to whites, parents with Ph.D.s to parents with no degree, all kinds of people from all different backgrounds across the country are choosing to homeschool.

Homeschooling Trends

The National Center for Education Statistics' research finds that parents choose to homeschool for a variety of reasons. Thirty-six percent do so "to provide religious or moral instruction." Twenty-one percent have concerns about the school environment, and 17% are not satisfied with the academic instruction. Other reasons include family time, finances, distance, and caring for a special needs child. [National Home Education Research Institute president Brian] Ray contends that there are even more reasons parents homeschool their children, citing a preference for a customized curriculum for each child, teaching methodology that is not provided in institutions, and enrichment of family relationships. [Researcher Eric] Isenberg adds to this list, mentioning the lack of private schools as yet another reason parents choose home-based education.

Modern-day homeschooling was begun in the 1970s by evangelicals. Initially, states treated homeschooling as a type of truancy.

More and more parents every year are choosing to homeschool their children. It is a trend that has grown tremendously in the last two decades. From 1991 to 1999, the number of homeschooled children almost tripled, going from 300,000 to 805,000, in the span of just eight years. In the United States today, the number of children being educated in the home is estimated to be between 1.2 and 2 million, which is significantly higher than the number of students enrolled in the New York City public school system. This number also exceeds the total of those enrolled in both charter schools and voucher programs throughout the country. Data from the National Center for Education Statistics also demonstrates a steady rise in home-based education from 1999 to 2007. In addition to those currently enrolled in home-based education, many public and private school students were homeschooled for part of their education when they were younger, which lends itself to a tendency illustrated through several studies from 2003 to 2007; it is more common to homeschool young children. Even very well educated mothers have difficulty providing quality academic instruction after the age of 11 as the subject matter becomes more complex.

The trend of homeschooling has prompted futuristic schools of thought, incorporating technological advancement into the trend itself; "In 2014 K–12 [kindergarten through grade twelve] education will no longer be confined to four walls and a classroom. Education will take place in a variety of settings, including Cyberspace and virtual reality [according to Robert Sanborn et al.]. Computers become classrooms, and software serves to grade papers and keep records. Isenberg concurs, stating that technological progress advances home-based education and has contributed to a homeschooling growth spurt. Sanborn et al., take their futuristic scenario a step further, alleging that homeschooling will become a kind of status symbol by the year 2014 and that mothers who homeschool will be seen as "highly sophisticated" and will be the "ideal of contemporary motherhood."

Homeschooling Implications

Critics charge that the homeschooling movement is detrimental in three ways; they allege that it is academically harmful, socially harmful, and that it upsets the public school system. Since home-based education is relatively new and difficult to assess in an experimental group of a significant number of students, there has been limited research in the area of homeschooling due to the lack of data. However, there are studies that provide strong evidence against these claims. Several demonstrate that homeschooled students normally score considerably higher on standardized achievement tests than public school students. They also do as well or better on measures of social and emotional development, and some research illustrates exceptional strength in the area of leadership. As for harm to the public school system, the argument is that education in the home draws resources away from the public schools: however, it also lightens the load of the state by making classes a little smaller and using less of the public schools supplies as counties are not obligated by law to allocate funds for homeschooling, while charter schools and vouchers, for example, do draw from public funds.

One comprehensive, specific way to measure the implications of homeschooling on an individual and societal level is to consider the transitional experiences of first-year college students who were homeschooled. There is not much research on this subject to date, but one investigation of this transitional path shows favorable results in virtually all areas for every student who participated in the study. The experiment, which was based on the five factors of achievement, leadership, professional aptitude, social behavior, and physical activity, illustrates "little difference in the areas of achievement, professional aptitude, social behavior, and physical activity based upon the school environment" [according to Mary Beth Bolle et al.] In the dimension of leadership, however, home-schooled students far exceed those educated in both public and private schools. Ray lends support to this finding, asserting that adults who were homeschooled were instilled with "self-concept leadership, self-esteem, and participate in community service." He also argues that they are more active in fulfilling their civic duty than the general population, and are extremely likely to internalize the belief system of their parents.

From Homeschooling to College

From the students' perspectives, the transition proves to be a tremendous learning experience, much in the same way that it is for their traditionally educated peers: they are both nervous and

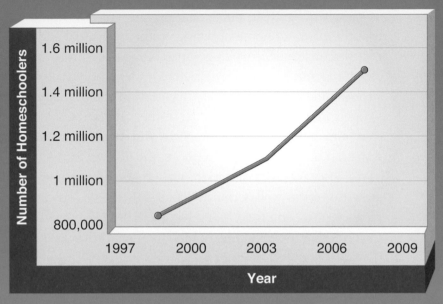

Estimated Number of US Homeschoolers, 1999–2007

Number of Homeschoolers

1.6 million
1.4 million
1.2 million
1 million
800,000

1997   2000   2003   2006   2009

Year

Taken from: "Fast Facts—Home Schooling." National Center for Educational Statistics.

eager to leave home and begin college; although they initially experience periods of loneliness, they are able to make friends quickly and they have to adjust their study habits to coincide with more challenging courses and a greater workload. The differences, though, are apparent as well. The students admit that meeting and spending time with people whose values are much different from their own is sometimes difficult and character building. They also mention the necessity to acclimate to traditional academics and different teaching styles. Some of the participants in the study missed their family and siblings significantly and took somewhat longer to form an "identity away from home" [as cited by Bolle et al.] than students with a background in traditional education, while, on the other hand, some were thrilled to have a break from the family and be relinquished of chores like changing diapers.

In all, research concludes that home-educated students go through the three stages of separation, transition, and incorporation in their move from home to college in a very similar fashion as those who study in public and private schools, which indicates that the effects of homeschooling on the individual and society are of little consequence when compared to those of traditionally educated students. In some ways, such as leadership and self confidence, strong evidence suggests that education in the home may create a stronger foundation. As a whole, studies on homeschooling concur that homeschooling is advantageous and should be part of our society as a school choice. Furthermore, the United States is not alone in this endeavor. Other nations are experiencing a homeschooling growth spurt as well. Countries like Australia, Canada, Hungary, Japan, Kenya, and the United Kingdom are just some of the other societies that are including home-based education as an option for the education of their citizens.

Homeschooling is a trend that continues to grow on a yearly basis. Legal, modern day home-based education is still new and, in some ways, experimental. Research shows that families choose to homeschool for a variety of reasons, and that the endeavor is an enormous undertaking of money, time and effort. Although families work together to provide better and higher levels of instruction, most parents who homeschool also use public or private schools. Since families typically rely on dual incomes, home-based education will probably not grow indefinitely, but will remain a viable school option for many parents. Although limited, research appears to indicate that homeschoolers can and do compete academically and socially with their traditionally educated peers, and that adults who were homeschooled are successful in the "real world." Finally, while it is impossible to predict all of the implications that homeschooling may have in the years to come, the evidence maintains that it does have a place in society. Hill insists, "In a situation where so little is understood, the potential harms of homeschooling seem far smaller than the harms of trying to prevent it or thwart it."

TWO

Homeschooling Is Increasing Among the Wealthy

Alexandra Jacobs

Homeschooling has dramatically increased in the United States over the last three decades. While some might assume the typical homeschoolers are conservative Christians with large families, homeschooling has also taken root among very wealthy families. Alexandra Jacobs, an editor at large for the *New York Observer*, explores the trend in the following viewpoint. Jacobs describes these homeschoolers, their parents, and homeschool co-ops. She also explains why these parents have turned to homeschooling and how they ensure that their children have broad experiences with diverse places and people.

Knock, knock. Who's there? Boo! Boo who? Boo hoo, don't cry you!

Under the shade of a fragrant pine tree in the backyard of a Clinton Hill, Brooklyn, brownstone one balmy morning in early June, a quartet of 4-year-olds is being schooled in a classic joke form by Krista, a black-clad brunette in her 20s with an onyx pendant dangling around her neck and an air of preternatural calm.

"We have a book, 'How Full Is Your Bucket?'" Krista tells a visitor. Then she turns to the class: "We all have an invisible bucket, and it gets full when we feel happy, and when it gets empty, how do we feel?"

"Very sad," replies one of the students, the golden-haired Fiona, who is wearing a dress in a fetching print of frogs and flowers, accessorized with lavender Crocs. Nearby, along with fallen hydrangea blossoms and a few matted paintbrushes, the ground bears the crumby evidence of a recent binge on Annie's Cheddar Bunnies, the organic-living set's retort to Pepperidge Farm Goldfish.

"So how do we fill up other people's buckets?" A Norah Jones song from a neighbor's stereo is wafting gently over the fence.

"By being happy!" says Theo, a cherub in army fatigues.

"And how do you fill up my bucket? How do I get really, really happy? When everyone's being—"

"Kind!" shouts young Mia, resplendent in blue leggings, a pink oxford-cloth shirt and fuchsia toenail polish under her Salt-Water sandals. "I love you, I love you, I love you," she adds by way of example.

Reasons to Homeschool

"Thank you, that makes me feel *sooo* happy," Krista says before turning to a lesson about bees and their hives. Her fourth charge, a quiet towhead in white T-shirt and jeans, is named Sonny, which a visitor first thought was spelled "Sunny." This is understandable, as it all seemed like sweetness and light at the Mini-R.A.D., short for Revolutionary Artistic Development: a fledgling home school cooperative started by the fashion photographers Tom Betterton and Jenny Gage three years ago [in 2007] with three other sets of Brooklyn hipster parents (a cinematographer, a dancer-choreographer and a sculptor among them) when the local schools didn't quite pass muster. Meanwhile, a small, customized school founded in 2007 by members of the Blue Man Group—attended by the offspring of various magazine editors and photographers—thrives in NoHo, in what could be called

"Hello, Johnny. I'm Tom, your shoe tying consultant, and this is Anne, your cereal planner."

"Hello, Johnny. I'm Tom, your shoe tying consultant, and this is your cereal planner," cartoon by Steamy Raimon. www.CartoonStock.com.

a burgeoning micromovement. New York City private schools are vexingly exclusive, after all, and passing through the public-school bureaucracy can feel like an outtake from [poet] Shel Silverstein's "Boa Constrictor" (also on Krista's lesson plan this morning). Since the city's bobos are now making their own pickles and ice cream, why not mold little minds as well?

Across the street, in the corner of a cozy, colorful classroom housed on the garden level of Betterton and Gage's own brownstone, the couple's son Leroy, 6—Sonny's older brother—is lolling on a queen-size mattress with four of his peers, who are listening with varied levels of attention as a tattooed tutor in round, horn-rimmed glasses and a pixie haircut reads aloud from "Charlie and the Chocolate Factory."

"He must watch television?" asks one of the pupils, incredulous at the idiot-box-obsessed Mike Teavee. Calderesque mobiles hang from the ceilings; a table is covered with bins of wrapping paper and rubber bands; on the (salvaged) door to the classroom, printed in vintage bronze, are the words LOST AND FOUND. Outside, on a vegetable plot tended with help from the R.A.D.'s fathers— "I'd say they are 50 percent as involved as the mothers," one of the latter says tolerantly—there is enough produce to stock the salad bar at Souplantation: kale, Swiss chard, carrots, broccoli and arugula.

"They eat well," Gage says, sitting in a ground-floor office on another school day as Betterton clusters around a computer with a few of the couple's photography assistants. "Sushi. They love sushi." Eight months pregnant with the couple's third child, a girl, she is the epitome of the glamour mama, utterly lacking the whiff of patchouli one might associate with the home-schooling movement.

The Growth of Homeschooling

"It's funny to me that it's come into vogue," says Marina Trejo, a Pilates instructor based in Williamsburg who has come across several home-schoolers in her practice. According to the United States Department of Education, an estimated 1.5 million children in grades K–12 [kindergarten through twelve] were home-educated in 2007, many of them for religious reasons; that number grew an average of 11 percent between 1999 and 2007. Trejo, who hails from San Diego, was taught with her siblings in a somewhat free-style manner during the 1980s by her mother, who had become radicalized at Berkeley. (Still, Trejo says, there were many afternoons of "I Love Lucy" reruns.) "It was incredibly uncommon, shocking," she says. "We were like walking monks. Going grocery shopping, there were comments like 'Why aren't you in school?'"

Gage was also raised in California (Malibu) and attended public school until 10th grade, when she went to boarding school;

Betterton grew up in Lawrenceville, N.J. Their educational brain wave struck after one of their au pairs took Leroy on a series of field trips. "He'd come home superinspired, talking about space and planets," she says. "His imagination just seemed to be exploding."

Meanwhile, the options available in hyper-stressed New York seemed unappealing. "Watching people go into school, the amount of difficulty and anxiety. . . ," Betterton says, trailing off with a grimace. "We just saw it as a new way of educating our kids."

Homeschooling Co-Op

The R.A.D.'s founding members contributed about $5,000 each toward a teacher's salary and the use of their homes, which rotated weekly at first. As their broods grew and other families signed on, the number of classes expanded to three. "The younger groups, you can't keep up with the number of people who want to be doing it," Betterton says. "When you start to approach kindergarten, people are really feeling that pressure: 'I gotta get my kid into something!'"

"It's all fun and games until first grade," Gage adds darkly. That's when official papers need to be filed with the Department of Education: a letter of intent; an Individualized Home Instruction Plan (IHIP); quarterly reports; and the results of an annual assessment. Lessons in arithmetic, reading, spelling, writing, English, geography, history, science, health ed, music, art and phys ed are required for first through sixth grades; the Betterton-Gages are resolved to continue at least through third.

"It's a lot of work," Betterton says, "but it's awesome. Because of the safe environment, the kids are insanely empathetic. In the classroom and outside, they somehow internalize an idea that they are involved in their own education, and also that they're involved in the education of the kids that they're learning with. They help each other out a lot. They all work together to support each other, and I don't see that happening as much in bigger, more hectic classrooms."

Children perform during the Blue Man Group workshop at a charter school in Washington, D.C. The workshops were begun in 2007 by members of the Blue Man Group, a performance art troupe.

The Social Diversity Question

But what of the socioeconomic diversity such classrooms afford, and the oft-leveled charge that home schooling isolates children in a privileged bubble of their parents' making? "It's hard," Betterton concedes. "It's a self-selecting group of people. But that's one of the reasons we are constantly outside in the world." Their frequent field trips include Governors Island, the American Museum of Natural History and the Mast Brothers Chocolate Factory in Williamsburg—Hershey Chocolate World it ain't—many of these outings lovingly documented in lush color on the school's blog. (The annual class photos are in black and white).

"People say, 'Are they socialized? And we say, 'They are *so* socialized,'" Gage says.

"These kids are everywhere, all the time," Betterton says.

Indeed, today they appear to be visiting France. Back in the classroom, Leroy and his fellow students are jumping up and down excitedly on a colorful blanket as a French teacher in a gingham frock recites a lesson.

"*Est-ce que tu es content, Leroy? Tu es triste?*" [Are you happy, Leroy? Are you sad?]

"*Content!*"

Two mothers, including the dancer-choreographer Cynthia Stanley, who helped oversee the school's Christmas recital, "A Totally Radical Nutcracker," look on with rapt approval. "We really stress trying to make sure that it's all hands-on, integrated studies—what's the other word that we were using?" Gage says.

Experiential Learning

"Experiential," chimes in one of the moms, Sarah Rogenes, a knitwear designer. "So if they're learning about measurements, they're not going to be doing worksheets. They're at the park measuring things or weighing things or cooking."

"It's so interesting when we go to a museum and see this mass herd of kids that are coming in from a public or private school, and how the kids are taking in content," Stanley says. "Because they're herding these kids, and they're getting great experiences, but it's just very different from the kids pondering and talking and asking the docent questions."

But is this a school, or artists trying to render a New York City childhood in perfect brush strokes?

"It's obviously gentrified more," Trejo says of the new home-schoolers. "Definitely more from people who have a privileged background, with one parent who has the luxury of working from home, which is not an option for a lot of working-class families."

Then again, she admits, "My son is going to a public pre-K [pre-kindergarten] in the fall, and I am somewhat terrified."

THREE

Homeschooling: The Sleeping Giant of American Education

Dan Lips and Evan Feinberg

Calling homeschooling "the sleeping giant of American education," Dan Lips, an educational analyst, and Evan Feinberg, a former research assistant in the Domestic Policy Studies Department at the Heritage Foundation, explain in this article why homeschooling in the United States has increased and is likely to keep increasing. Lips and Feinberg overview the growth of homeschooling, the success of the homeschooling rights movement, and homeschooling demographics. They argue that the successful outcomes of homeschooling include the academic achievement, college performance, and positive life outcomes of homeschoolers. They also assert that homeschooling will continue to grow due to increased support for homeschoolers in the form of publications, networks, public school cooperation, school-choice tax credits, and technology.

A growing number of American families are choosing to homeschool their children. According to the Department of Education's National Center for Education Statistics, approximately 850,000 students were being homeschooled in 1998. The National Home Education Research Institute indicates that number now stands at around 3,000,000.

Families cite common reasons for choosing to homeschool their offspring, such as concern about the environment of a designated school (85%), dissatisfaction with the academic instruction in a particular school system (68%), and a preference for religious and moral instruction not provided in traditional schools (72%).

The decentralized nature of the homeschooling population limits researchers' ability to draw conclusions about the specific effect of homeschooling on various outcome measures, such as academic achievement. However, evaluations of homeschooled students show they perform well in that academic environment. Moreover, a survey of adults who were homeschooled suggests that it leads to positive life outcomes, such as higher college attendance and enrollment.

The growing number of students being educated at home is influencing the American education system and saving taxpayers as much as $9,900,000,000 each year. The percentage of homeschooled students likely will continue to grow. Technological and societal trends may make homeschooling a viable option worth pursuing. Federal and state policymakers and the private sector have the ability to safeguard homeschooling and improve the opportunities for families to give their children the best possible education at home.

Homeschooling is an alternative form of education in which children are instructed at home rather than at a traditional public or private school. Youngsters are taught by parents, guardians, or other tutors. Historically, home education has been a primary method for parents to educate their children. Many of America's Founders were educated at home, including George Washington and Thomas Jefferson. Over time, the rise of compulsory education laws eroded the prevalence of home instruction. However, since the 1970s and 1980s, homeschooling gradually has become a popular method of instruction once again.

During this time, homeschooling advocates have pressed for the legal right to forgo compulsory school attendance and educate their children at home, but not without opposition. For instance, the National Education Association has advocated placing restrictions on homeschooling. At its 2007 annual meeting, it approved a resolution calling for tighter regulation of home-schooling: "When home schooling occurs . . . instruction should be by persons who are licensed by the appropriate state education licensure agency, and a curriculum approved by the state department of education should be used." However, such efforts to restrict or tightly regulate homeschooling largely have failed, as, at present, homeschooling is legal in every state.

The Home School Legal Defense Association (HSLDA), a nonprofit organization that advocates for homeschooling, rates the degree to which states regulate homeschooling. According to HSLDA, 10 states require no notice from homeschoolers; 15 have "low regulation" (requiring only parental notification); 19 have "moderate regulations"; and six states have "high regulation."

The establishment of legal homeschooling rights across the country has facilitated strong growth in the number of youngsters being educated at home. National Home Education Research Institute figures reveal that about 2,400,000 children were educated at home during the 2005–06 school year, and that the number of children being homeschooled grows seven to 12% per year.

A Department of Education survey provides background on homeschooling families. White students are more likely to be homeschooled than African-American or Hispanic pupils. Kids in two-parent families with only one parent in the workforce also are more likely to be homeschooled. Youngsters from families with annual household incomes below $75,000 were more likely to be homeschooled than those with families who earned more than that amount each year. Participation also was higher among families with at least one parent who had earned a college degree.

The decentralized nature of the homeschooling population makes it difficult to draw definitive conclusions about academic achievement and other outcomes. No controlled experiments have been conducted comparing the performance of home-schooled students with the performance of their peers in traditional schools. Without a controlled experiment, drawing definite conclusions about the effectiveness of homeschooling as a method of instruction compared to traditional schooling is impossible. However, a number of researchers have evaluated

Reasons Given for Homeschooling

While the single most frequent reason parents decide to homeschool their children involves religious or moral instruction, the majority of parents do not homeschool for religious reasons.

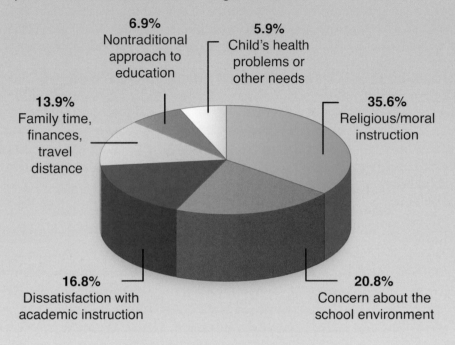

6.9%
Nontraditional approach to education

5.9%
Child's health problems or other needs

13.9%
Family time, finances, travel distance

35.6%
Religious/moral instruction

16.8%
Dissatisfaction with academic instruction

20.8%
Concern about the school environment

Taken from: US Department of Education, National Center for Education Statistics, 2009.

the performance of homeschoolers on various measures and have reported that these individuals seem to be doing well in their learning environment. Lawrence Rudner of the University of Maryland administered academic achievement tests to 20,760 homeschooled students. He reports that "the achievement tests of this group of homeschool students are exceptionally high—the median scores were typically in the 70th to 80th percentile." He also found that 25% of the homeschooled students tested are enrolled one or more grade levels above their age-level peers in traditional public or private schools. Rudner cautions that the results do not demonstrate that homeschooling is superior to public or private education, but he does state that the findings suggest that "homeschool students do quite well in the environment." Paul Jones and Gene Gloeckner published an evaluation of first-year college performance of homeschoolers and traditional public school students in *The Journal of College Admissions*. They summarized the available academic literature and reported that the evidence shows that homeschoolers perform as well as traditional public school students on college preparatory exams and in first-year college grade point averages. The researchers conducted their own experiment and found no statistical difference between homeschool graduates and traditional high school graduates on nine measures of college preparedness. "The academic performance analyses," conclude the authors, "indicate that homeschool graduates are as ready for college as traditional high school graduates and that they perform as well on national college assessment tests as traditional high school graduates."

Evidence also suggests that homeschoolers experience positive life outcomes compared to the general population. Brian Ray of the National Home Education Research Institute surveyed 7,300 adults (ages 18 through 24) who were homeschooled. Among the respondents, 74% had taken college-level courses, compared to 46% of the general population. They also were involved in their communities and engaged in civic affairs at higher rates than the average population. They were more likely to report being "happy" than was the general population. Although this survey is not a scientific measure, the results support the idea that homeschooling likely leads to similar or positive life outcomes compared to the general population.

Academic researchers have concluded that family background characteristics are a primary factor in shaping students' academic achievement. Homeschooling families are more likely to have at least one parent who earned a college degree compared to the general population, and homeschooled students are more likely to live in two-parent households.

The growing number of students being educated at home affects the public education system in a number of ways. Homeschooling saves taxpayers resources that otherwise would have been spent educating these children if they had enrolled in public school. Public education is financed through complex funding formulas and revenue streams that come from Federal, state, and local taxpayers. Determining the extent of savings from each homeschooled child is difficult. Generally, states fund schools through a formula system on a per student basis, but the Federal government and local government bodies do not provide funding on a per student basis. However, it is safe to say that, if the nation's approximately 3,000,000 homeschooled students chose to enroll in U.S. public schools for the 2009–10 academic year, states and communities would need to allocate significant funding to accommodate all of them.

The continued growth of the number of homeschooling families has led to a proliferation of resources and networks that facilitate the process. Twenty-five years ago, a family that wanted to homeschool would likely have had limited curriculum and instructional options. Today, the options are nearly boundless. An Internet search on "homeschooling" produces more than 13,000,000 hits. Parents can find and purchase curriculum materials through online exchanges and other networks. Hundreds of websites, blogs, and books are devoted to supporting parents who homeschool. In some cases, parents can access free or low-cost instructional products to teach their kids. Other options include online learning services that offer professionally developed courses for relatively low monthly fees. Across the U.S., a growing number of for-profit tutoring providers are in operation, allowing parents the opportunity to make available supplementary instruction for their children.

Parents also can join a growing number of homeschooling networks across the U.S. and around the world. Most states have some form of support network for homeschooling. They facilitate collaborative instruction and opportunities for socialization for homeschooled students. For instance, pupils can participate in speech and debate tournaments tailored to homeschooled students through the National Christian Forensics and Communications Association. Homeschoolers can take part in various athletic networks as well. Many states have policies that facilitate home instruction by allowing homeschoolers to participate in some public school activities. At least 20 states have policies established by statute or legal ruling that allow homeschooled students to take part in extracurricular activities and athletics.

Many public schools offer homeschooled students the opportunity to attend part time. The Education Commission of the States reports that encouraging these pupils to attend can lead to additional funding—as well as requirements that home-

Homeschooling saves taxpayers resources that otherwise would have been spent educating those children in public schools.

schooled individuals participate in state-mandated testing. In addition, a growing number of states offer some form of distance and online learning opportunities. According to the Department of Education, some 40% of public school districts have students enrolled in distance education courses. In all, over 10% of public schools nationwide—5% in rural communities—have distance education courses.

Education tax credits or deductions for qualifying education-related expenses are available in some states. Education tax credits and deductions reduce a taxpayer's tax liability or the amount of income that is subject to tax. For example, Iowa, Illinois, and Minnesota give various tax credits and deductions for education-related expenses, including private school tuition and payments for instructional materials. As education tax credits proliferate across the country, homeschooling could become, a more affordable option.

Other technological and societal trends also could contribute to continued growth in homeschooling. In the future, more families may be able to find creative ways to balance work and home responsibilities, potentially increasing the likelihood that they can homeschool their children. One promising trend is telecommuting. According to the U.S. Census Bureau, an estimated 5,000,000 Americans were working from home before the onset of the recession. The percentage of individuals who work from home has increased at twice the growth rate of the overall workforce.

Homeschooling is an important component of the student-centered educational reforms that are changing the landscape of American education. Millions of families benefit from greater opportunities to control how their children are educated through student-centered reforms. For instance, more than 150,000 children are attending private schools using publicly funded scholarships through private school-choice programs, and an estimated 1,200,000 students attend charter schools instead of traditional public schools.

The growing number of students taking advantage of school-choice options has created competition for the traditional public school system. The threat of losing students pressures public schools to reform in order to attract more students. Harvard University economist Caroline Hoxby, evaluating the competitive effects of school-choice programs in Arizona, Wisconsin, and Michigan, found that competition has caused public schools to improve performance. Whether the growing trend toward homeschooling is creating similar competition for other traditional public school systems is an interesting question for further academic research.

FOUR

Making Education History: Beyond the Status Quo

The Old Schoolhouse Magazine

> According to 2012 statistics from the US Department of Education, homeschooling is growing at a more rapid rate than enrollment in public schools (7 percent vs. 1 percent). The reason for this rapid growth is the success homeschoolers achieve, according to this viewpoint, which first appeared as an article for the *Old Schoolhouse Magazine*, a trade magazine for homeschoolers. The author argues that homeschooling is making education history in that homeschoolers score higher on standardized college entrance exams, are more likely to succeed in college, and are more likely to succeed socially and financially in adulthood than are their traditional-school counterparts.

With more than 2 million K–12 students in the U.S. currently being educated at home, the popularity of homeschooling continues to rise. Since 1999, the number of homeschooled students has increased by a staggering 75%, mostly in response to increasing dissatisfaction and frustration with the public school system.

Statistics from the U.S. Department of Education Recently documented less than a 1% increase in enrollment of K–12 public school students nationwide, but the homeschool population

The author claims the average expenditure for homeschooled children is $500 to $600 a year per child compared with the average of $10,000 per child per year for public school students.

increased by a whopping 7%. Almost 4% (and growing) of our nation's school-age children are being educated at home.

Research has proven that parents are more than capable of successfully educating their children at home. Surveys of home-schoolers' academic successes consistently reveal that they score, on average, at the 65th to 89th percentile on standardized academic achievement tests, compared to a national school average at the 50th percentile. Interestingly, according to a recent, nationwide survey of homeschoolers commissioned by the Home School Legal Defense Association (HSLDA), achievement gaps that are "well-documented in public school between boys and girls, parents with lower incomes, and parents with lower levels of education are not found among homeschoolers."

Recent studies laud homeschoolers' academic success, noting their significantly higher ACT-Composite scores as high schoolers and higher grade point averages as college students. Yet surprisingly, the average expenditure for the education of a homeschooled child, per year, is $500 to $600, compared to an average expenditure of $10,000 per child, per year, for public school students.

More than ever, homeschool grads are scoring points with college recruiters. Compared to the overall population of college students, homeschool grads achieve a higher retention rate and a higher graduation rate as they pursue education beyond the training provided by their parents. Dori Staehle, in her February 2012 article, notes that schools such as Harvard, Yale, MIT, Stanford, and Duke are actively recruiting homeschoolers—and offering them scholarships. She cites the characteristics of homeschoolers who have gotten their attention: "These students tend to be exceptionally bright, motivated, and mature. Far from being sheltered and shy (the typical stereotypes), homeschoolers' applications reflect students who have traveled, taken risks, and studied some pretty intense topics."

National Home Education Research Institute (NHERI) survey results confirm that homeschoolers are "engaged, at least as much as are others, in activities that predict leadership in adulthood" and are "satisfied that they were home educated." Homeschool graduates are more civically engaged than the general public and demonstrate "healthy social, psychological, and emotional development, and success into adulthood." Apparently homeschoolers are getting excellent grades on their report cards—both academically and socially!

Based on recent data, researchers such as Dr. Brian Ray "expect to observe a notable surge in the number of children being homeschooled in the next 5 to 10 years. The rise would be in terms of both absolute numbers and percentage of the K to 12 student population. This increase would be in part because . . . [1] a large number of those individuals who were being home educated in the 1990s may begin to homeschool their own school-age children and [2] the continued successes of home-educated students."

Dr. Gary Knowles, a professor at the University of Michigan, conducted a survey of homeschool grads who are now successful adults. He found that "an amazing 96% said if they could do it all over again they would want to be homeschooled. Not a single one was unemployed or on welfare. That is pretty impressive."

Homeschooling parents have chosen to educate their own kids at home for a myriad of reasons, and many say they are in it for the long haul. It's a matter of conviction and dedication. And,

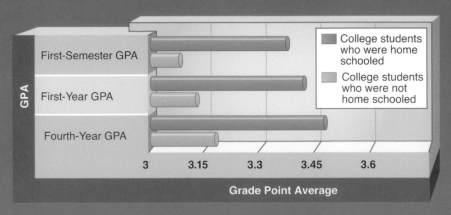

Homeschoolers and College Success

Compared to their counterparts, homeschoolers on average earn higher college grade point averages (GPAs).

College students who were home schooled

College students who were not home schooled

First-Semester GPA

First-Year GPA

Fourth-Year GPA

GPA

3   3.15   3.3   3.45   3.6

Grade Point Average

Taken from: Michael F. Corgan. "Exploring Academic Outcomes of Homeschooled Students." *Journal of College Admission*, Summer 2010, pp. 18–25.

judging from the current state of the public school system, the answer for thousands of parents in this country is clear and simple: homeschool them.

Are homeschoolers "making education history"? For sure. As did the homeschooling parents of individuals such as Abraham Lincoln, Booker T. Washington, Thomas Edison, Frank Lloyd Wright, and Andrew Wyeth, equipped with parental insight and motivation to see their children succeed academically and socially, today's homeschooling parents are making education history.

FIVE

Parents Have the Right to Homeschool Their Children

Michael Farris

Homeschooling advocates have worked hard to secure the rights of homeschoolers, and the success of homeschoolers both academically and socially has validated their efforts, according to Michael Farris, a constitutional lawyer and a founder of the Home School Legal Defense Association. In the following viewpoint he cautions that the fight for homeschooling rights is not yet over and names "academic elites" as the adversary because they seek to regulate homeschooling and they accuse homeschooling advocates of intolerance. Farris argues that these academic elites are hypocritical because they seek to use totalitarian methods to enforce tolerance.

The shades were drawn. Children did not play outside from 8 in the morning until 3 in the afternoon. Moms did not run to the store with kids in tow during those same hours. If a deliveryman knocked on the front door with a package, the children scrambled into a back room while Mom answered the door. Not every homeschooler behaved this way in the 1980s, but many did. It was a scary time in many places and in many ways.

In those days the education establishment had two things to say about homeschooling: (1) Parents were unqualified to deliver appropriate academic content and (2) Children would not be properly socialized if they were homeschooled. Both of those assertions have been proven wrong over time.

Certainly there are those in the education establishment who continue to mutter these lines under their breath while begrudgingly acquiescing to the fact that homeschooling exists and it is legal. But no one believes that such arguments will ever prevail again in our lifetimes. The reason this is true is that the general public has become convinced that homeschooling works well both academically and socially.

One of the criticisms of evangelical schooling is that it teaches intolerance of other religions.

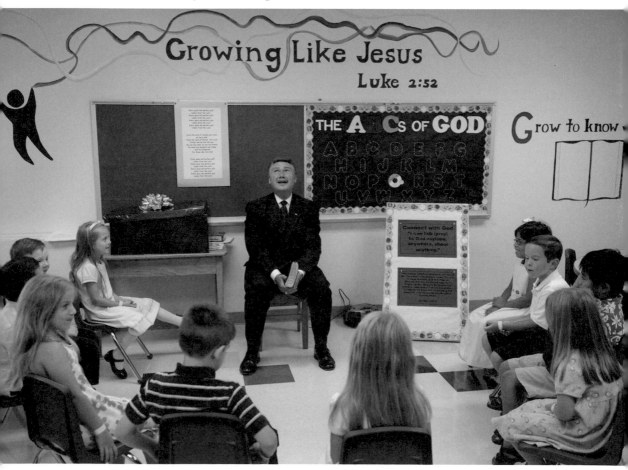

This public acceptance has been won at a considerable price and homeschoolers need to protect that reputation. One way to ensure that it is protected is that homeschool speakers and leaders need to ensure that when they are giving their "sales pitch" to a potential homeschooling parent that they do not understate the amount of hard work that it takes to be very successful. Our

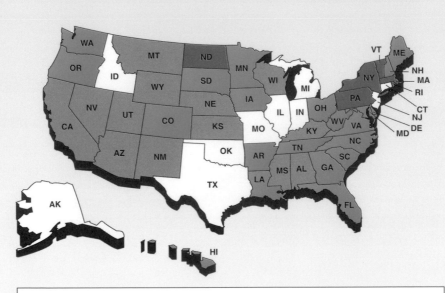

State Laws for Homeschool Regulation

States requiring no notice: No state requirement for parents to initiate any contact.

States with low regulation: State requires parental notification only.

States with moderate regulation: State requires parents to send notification, test scores, and/or professional evaluation of student progress.

States with high regulation: State requires parents to send notification or achievement test scores and/or professional evaluation, plus other requirements (e.g., curriculum approval by the state, teacher qualification of parents, or home visits by state officials).

Taken from: "State Laws." Home School legal Defense Association. www.hslda.org/laws/.

message should be: Yes, it does require sacrifice, but at the end of the day the rewards far outweigh the sacrifice.

The Voices Against Homeschooling

Just as society has grown accustomed to the legitimacy of homeschooling, the elites—especially the academic elites—have decided to take direct aim at our movement.

A growing number of scholars and professors are alarmed by the growth of the Christian homeschooling movement. Perhaps their alarm grows out of their exposure to an increasing number of homeschooled graduates who make their way into the highest echelons of college education. While such professors have been able to modify the convictions of decades of professing Christians who arrive at their institutions, it is likely that they are finding that Christian homeschooled students are more difficult to convert to their secular-socialist mindsets.

While we cannot know for sure about their personal experiences, the scholarly journal pieces such professors have written leave no doubt as to their fierce opinions. These academic elites want to crush the Christian homeschooling movement.

Robert Reich of Stanford, Kimberly Yuracko of Northwestern University, and Catherine Ross of George Washington University have all published calls for dramatic regulation of the substantive content of home education. They believe that we are intolerant.

In what way are we intolerant? They correctly understand that Christian homeschoolers teach our children that Jesus meant what He said when He proclaimed, "I am the way the truth and the life, no man cometh unto the Father but by Me." The flip-side of that truth is that all other religions are false.

If we would say that Jesus is one of the many ways to God—assuming for the purposes of discussion that there really is a God—then we would be acceptable in the eyes of these elites. But because we make a stand for the One who is Truth, we are labeled intolerant.

The Threat of Totalitarianism

And what should be done about our intolerance? Listen to Catherine Ross:

> Many liberal political theorists argue, however, that there are limits to tolerance. In order for the norm of tolerance to survive across generations, society need not and should not tolerate the inculcation of absolutist views that undermine toleration of difference.

Yeah, that is what she really said. Ross & Co. are willing to use totalitarian tactics to establish their regime of tolerance.

If you doubt this, listen to the even more shrill voice of Martha Albertson Fineman of Emory University:

> The more appropriate suggestion for our current educational dilemma is that public education should be mandatory and universal. Parental expressive interest could supplement but never supplant the public institutions where the basic and fundamental lesson would be taught and experienced by all American children: we must struggle together to define ourselves both as a collective and as individuals.

To ensure tolerance, Fineman advocates banning all private education so that coercive lessons of inclusion and diversity can be taught in the lockstep uniformity of public schools.

It is a wonder that these people do not implode from their internal inconsistencies.

We should not think that these issues are isolated or these opinions do not matter. The New Hampshire Supreme Court recently ruled that an 11-year-old girl could no longer be homeschooled because they wanted her to learn the lessons of diversity and tolerance in public schools. The brief filed by this girl's father cites the articles by Yuracko and Ross and others of this persuasion in his successful attempt to get this court to deny the right of home education.

We dare not think that the battle for our liberty has been won. The other side is gearing up for the fight of a generation. We need to meet them prepared and willing to once again use our rights as citizens to preserve our God-given roles as parents.

SIX

Homeschooling Violates Progressive Liberal Values

Dana Goldstein

> With homeschooling becoming more widely accepted and practiced among both conservatives and liberals, Dana Goldstein explores in the following viewpoint whether or not homeschooling supports progressive liberal values—in particular whether or not homeschooling is good for society at large, not just for individual families. Goldstein explores this question in the context of critiquing an essay by filmmaker Astra Taylor, who was homeschooled herself and supports homeschooling. She concludes that homeschooling does not support progressive values because the foundation of homeschooling is fear of society, and the practice of homeschooling would not be possible without class privilege. Goldstein further argues that homeschooling comes with social costs.

As a child growing up in Arizona and Georgia college towns during the 1980s and 1990s, the filmmaker Astra Taylor was "unschooled" by her lefty, countercultural parents. "My siblings and I slept late and never knew what day of the week it was," Taylor writes in a new essay in the literary journal *N+1*. "We were

never tested, graded, or told to memorize dates, facts, or figures.
. . . Some days we read books, made music, painted, or drew. Other
days we argued and fought over the computer. Endless hours were
spent watching reruns of 'The Simpsons' on videotape, though we
had every episode memorized. When we weren't inspired—which
was often—we simply did nothing at all."

Over the past year, there has been a resurgence of interest
in homeschooling—not just the religious fundamentalist variety
practiced by [Minnesota congresswoman] Michele Bachman and
[former US senator] Rick Santorum, but also in secular, liberal
homeschooling like Taylor's. Think no textbooks, history lessons
about progressive social movements, and college-level math for
precocious 13-year-olds. Some families implement this vision on
their own, while others join cooperatives of like-minded, super-
involved parents.

Homeschooling is so unevenly regulated from state to state that
it is impossible to know exactly how many homeschoolers there
are. Estimates range from about 1 million to 2 million children,
and the number is growing. It is unclear how many homeschooling families are secular, but the political scientist Rob Reich has
written that there is little doubt the homeschooling population
has diversified in recent years. Yet whether liberal or conservative,
"[o]ne article of faith unites all homeschoolers: that homeschooling should be unregulated," Reich writes. "Homeschoolers of all
stripes believe that they alone should decide how their children
are educated."

Liberal Homeschooling

Could such a go-it-alone ideology ever be truly progressive—by
which I mean, does homeschooling serve the interests not just of
those who are doing it, but of society as a whole?

In her *N+1* piece, Taylor struggles to answer this question
in the affirmative. Drawing upon her own upbringing, as well
as on the traditions of the radical private school the Albany
Free School, Taylor calls on parents and students to "empty the
schools," which force students to endure "irrational authority six

Family Income: Homeschooling Versus Non-Homeschooling Families, 2007

Fewer poor families homeschool their children.

Homeschooling Families

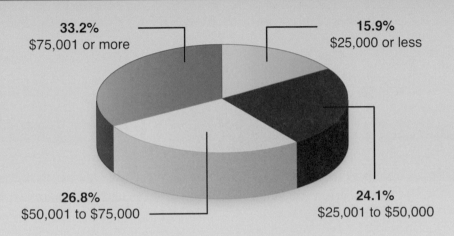

33.2%
$75,001 or more

15.9%
$25,000 or less

26.8%
$50,001 to $75,000

24.1%
$25,001 to $50,000

Non-Homeschooling Families

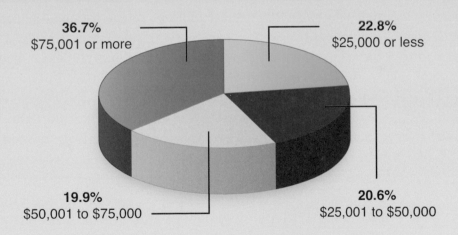

36.7%
$75,001 or more

22.8%
$25,000 or less

19.9%
$50,001 to $75,000

20.6%
$25,001 to $50,000

Taken from: US Census Bureau. "Students Who Are Homeschooled by Selected Characteristics: 2007." Statistical Abstract, 2012.

and a half hours a day, five days a week, in a series of cinder-block holding cells," she caricatures.

This overheated hostility toward public schools runs throughout the new literature on liberal homeschooling, and reveals what is so fundamentally illiberal about the trend: It is rooted in distrust of the public sphere, in class privilege, and in the dated presumption that children hail from two-parent families, in which at least one parent can afford (and wants) to take significant time away from paid work in order to manage a process—education—that most parents entrust to the community at-large.

Distrust of the Public Sphere

Take, for instance, Sonia Songha's *New York Times* account of forming a preschool cooperative with six other brownstone-Brooklyn mothers, all of whom "said our children had basically never left our sides." Indeed, in a recent *Newsweek* report, the education journalist Linda Perlstein noted a significant number of secular homeschoolers are also adherents of attachment parenting, the perennially controversial ideology defined by practices such as co-sleeping with one's child and breast-feeding for far longer than typical, sometimes well beyond toddlerhood. Meanwhile, in suburban New Jersey, one "hippy" homeschooler told the local paper she feared exposing her kids to the presumably negative influences of teachers and peers. "I didn't want my child being raised by someone else for eight hours out of the day," she said.

Recent reports of teachers and teachers' aides in Los Angeles and New York molesting children only fan the flames of such fears. But these stories make news exactly because they are so rare; there's something creepy about giving in totally to the terrors of the outside world harming one's child. In a country increasingly separated by cultural chasms—Christian conservatives vs. secular humanists; Tea Partiers vs. Occupiers—should we really encourage children to trust only their parents or those hand-selected by them, and to mistrust civic life and public institutions?

Moreover, being your child's everything—her parent, teacher, baby-sitter, and afterschool program coordinator—requires a massive outlay of labor. Songha's pre-K [pre-kindergarten] cooperative hired a teacher, but parents ended up putting in 10 to 12 hours of work per week administrating the program. Astra Taylor's father was a college professor, while her mother supervised the four children's "unschooling."

Class Privilege

What goes unmentioned is what made this lifestyle possible: the fact that Taylor's mother could afford to stay home with her kids. Yet Taylor bristles against the suggestion that there was anything unique about the ability of her upper-middle class, uber-intellectual parents to effectively "unschool" their children while still helping them grow into educated adults with satisfying professional lives. This critique "implies that most people are not gifted, and that they need to be guided, molded, tested, and inspected," Taylor complains. "What makes us so sure most people couldn't handle self-education?"

What makes us so sure? Reality. More than 70 percent of mothers with children under the age of 18 are in the workforce. One-third of all children and one-half of low-income children are being raised by a single parent. Fewer than one-half of young children, and only about one-third of low-income kids, are read to daily by an adult. Surely, this isn't the picture of a nation ready to "self-educate" its kids.

The Social Costs

Nor can we allow homeschoolers to believe their choice impacts only their own offspring. Although the national school-reform debate is fixated on standardized testing and "teacher quality"—indeed, the uptick in secular homeschooling may be, in part, a backlash against this narrow education agenda—a growing body of research suggests "peer effects" have a large impact on student achievement. Low-income kids earn higher test scores when they attend school alongside middle-class kids, while the test scores of privileged children are impervious to the influence of less-privileged peers. So when college-educated parents pull their kids

Dana Goldstein (at microphone) believes that homeschooling does not support progressive values because the foundation of homeschooling is class privilege and fear of society.

out of public schools, whether for private schooling or home-schooling, they make it harder for less-advantaged children to thrive.

Of course, no one wants to sacrifice his own child's education in order to better serve someone else's kid. But here's the great thing about attending racially and socioeconomically integrated schools: It helps children become better grown-ups. Research by Columbia University sociologist Amy Stuart Wells found that adult graduates of integrated high schools shared a commitment to diversity, to understanding and bridging cultural differences, and to appreciating "the humanness of individuals across racial lines."

Taylor admits that "[m]any people, liberal and conservative alike, are deeply offended by critiques of compulsory schooling." I suppose I am one of them. I benefited from 13 years of public education in one of the most diverse and progressive school districts in the United States. My father, stepmother, stepfather, and grandfather are or were public school educators. As an education journalist, I've admired many public schools that use culturally relevant, high-standards curricula to engage even the most disadvantaged students. These schools are sustained by the talents of impossibly hard-working teachers who want to partner with parents and kids, not oppress them.

Flood the Schools

Despite our conflicting perspectives, I agree with Taylor that school ought to be more engaging, more intellectually challenging, and less obsessed with testing. But government is the only institution with the power and scale to intervene in the massive undertaking of better educating American children, 90 percent of whom currently attend public schools. (And it's worth remembering that schools provide not just education, but basic child care while parents are at work.) Lefty homeschoolers might be preaching sound social values to their children, but they aren't practicing them. If progressives want to improve schools, we shouldn't empty them out. We ought to flood them with our kids, and then debate vociferously what they ought to be doing.

SEVEN

Homeschooling Does Not Violate Progressive Liberal Values

Conor Friedersdorf

> The following viewpoint by Conor Friedersdorf, a journalist and staff writer for the *Atlantic*, is a direct response to Dana Goldstein's 2012 article in which she argues that homeschooling violates progressive liberal values because it is not good for society at large and is easier for wealthier families. Friedersdorf argues that Goldstein's argument fails altogether because society and students benefit from the diversity of different types of educational environments. He asserts that homeschooling should remain an educational choice alongside many other educational choices.

In a controversial *Slate* article published last week [February 16, 2012], the talented education journalist Dana Goldstein laments what she says is the go-it-alone ideology of homeschooling parents, arguing that they harm children in the public school system and do society as a whole a disservice. "In a country increasingly separated by cultural chasms—Christian conservatives vs. secular humanists; Tea Partiers vs. Occupiers—should we really encourage children to trust only their parents or those hand-selected by them," she asks, "and to mistrust civic life and public institutions?"

She goes on:

Although the national school-reform debate is fixated on standardized testing and "teacher quality"—indeed, the uptick in secular homeschooling may be, in part, a backlash against this narrow education agenda—a growing body of research suggests "peer effects" have a large impact on student achievement. Low-income kids earn higher test scores when they attend school alongside middle-class kids, while the test scores of privileged children are impervious to the influence of less-privileged peers. So when college-educated parents pull their kids out of public schools, whether for private school or homeschooling, they make it harder for less-advantaged children to thrive.

. . . [N]o one wants to sacrifice his own child's education in order to better serve someone else's kid. But here's the great thing about attending racially and socioeconomically integrated schools: It helps children become better grown-ups. Research by Columbia University sociologist Amy Stuart Wells found that adult graduates of integrated high schools shared a commitment to diversity, to understanding and bridging cultural differences, and to appreciating "the humanness of individuals across racial lines.

Fallacies in Goldstein's Argument

Before addressing the core failures of this argument, its useful to run through some of its smaller inadequacies:

- The fact that a child is home-schooled doesn't mean he or she is being told to trust only his or her parent.
- Families that homeschool or send their kids to private school pay into the public school system just like every other local taxpayer, but their kids aren't a burden on its resources. Were everyone to attend public schools instead, would the "peer effect," if it exists, be significant enough to outweigh the extra cost of educating all the homeschoolers and private school kids?

- Are the test scores of low-income students really a reliable measure of how much they're thriving?
- Amy Stuart Wells was writing about the Class of 1980. Since cultural attitudes about diversity have radically changed in the intervening years, isn't it possible that the effect of attending a diverse high school is less pronounced?
- If all we know about integrated high schools is that their graduates are more committed to diversity and better able to bridge cultural differences—good things, to be sure—can we really conclude that these graduates are "better grown-ups" than graduates of less diverse high schools? Hypothetically, what if a less diverse private school produced graduates who were more academically prepared, more committed to gender equality, and more adept at problem solving that brought about social improvements? What if a homeschool collective meanwhile produced graduates who were more inclined to forgive their enemies, more likely to give to charity, and more likely to volunteer abroad? Judging what schools produce "better grown-ups" is thorny. Doing so by citing three diversity metrics in a vacuum is absurd.

None of these objections explains why I am so antagonistic to the notion that everyone should join the public school system. I'm glad it's there. I want it to be well-funded and substantially improved. I presume a majority of Americans will always attend public schools. But I value diversity more highly than Goldstein or [blogger] Freddie deBoer, however often they invoke that same word. In their vision, kids from different races and classes should come together in a public school system that everyone in America is invested in improving. I agree. But I want alternatives to exist too.

There are several compelling reasons why.

Diverse Needs

One reason is that individuals have different needs. Think back to your school days. I'm sure you remember people in your class who thrived, and others who'd have learned more and been happier in

Noted educator and political progressive Friedrich Hayek thought that a diversified educational system that included competitive models against which to measure public schools was good for education.

a different environment. Perhaps an all girls school. Or a military academy. Or a homeschool. You'd think people attuned to the diversity of kids in America would grasp that the public school system is never going to be set up in a way that is best suited to all of them, no matter how successfully it is reformed, or how many resources are poured into constantly improving it. Hurray if public schools exist *alongside other options* where some students flourish, for those other options accommodate difference far better than a single universalist model.

The Social Benefits

Society benefits from institutional diversity too. Goldstein writes, "I benefited from 13 years of public education in one of the most diverse and progressive school districts in the United States. My father, stepmother, stepfather, and grandfather are or were public school educators." Says deBoer, "What I learned by coming up, K–12 [kindergarten through grade twelve], surrounded by children who were not like me on many dimensions was that this

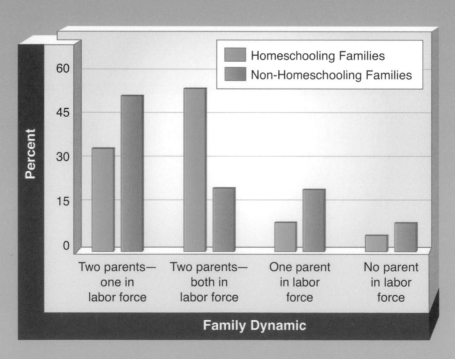

Parents in the Workforce: Homeschooling Versus Non-Homeschooling Families, 2007

Taken from: US Census Bureau. "Students Who Are Homeschooled by Selected Characteristics: 2007." Statistical Abstract, 2012.

diversity is in and of itself the best education." They seem curiously blind to the fact that many attendees of private schools and homeschooling collectives can speak as eloquently about unique things *they* learned at school. The Catholic school system, where I was educated, soured me on the faith, but I was able to glean substantial wisdom from the Catholic perspective on the world, and I'd doubtless have learned a different set of valuable lessons had I been educated by Hindus or Muslims or [filmmaker] Alan Jacobs.

Would these different sorts of wisdom all survive if an increasingly centralized public school system operated as a monopoly? Aren't we better off in a society that draws on folks who got different sorts of education? Some progressives seem to think a diverse society is one where every 14-year-old in America arrives at school, pledges allegiance to the nation's flag, takes out an American history textbook shaped by panels of bureaucrats in California and Texas, and proceeds to be guided by a teacher with a state issued credential in how best to pass a standardized test. Who is celebrating diversity, the champions of putting every kid in the education wonk's vision of the ideal classroom, or the folks who want some kids to start their day interacting with multiethnic classmates while others start their school day praying and still others learn about raising backyard chickens?

The Best Education

The final question is what sort of educational system is likely to produce the best results in the long run, or to be more specific, what system is best suited to evolving in advantageous ways. I'd bet on the diversified system, the one where there are always competitors with different models to measure public schools against. As [liberal philosopher] Friedrich Hayek put it, there is value in

> rules which are neither coercive nor deliberately imposed—
> rules which, though observing them is regarded as merit and
> though they will be observed by the majority, can be broken
> by individuals who feel that they have strong enough reasons

to brave the censure of their fellows. . . . Rules of this kind allow for gradual and experimental change. The existence of individuals and groups simultaneously observing partially different rules provides the opportunity for the selection of the more effective ones.

This philosophy suggests a different message for homeschooling parents than the one Goldstein offers. It might go something like this:

There is value in the public education system. Lots of intelligent, informed people have helped to shape its curriculum and norms. Consider their model with an open mind, and depart from it only after taking their claims seriously. And if you reach an informed conclusion that a different model is better, if that is your strong conviction, go out and be the change you want to see in the world. It may happen that you're right or wrong, but society as a whole requires people who challenge the prevailing system if it is to identify the few who can offer new insights.

This approach ought to be particularly appealing to dissident cultural critics like deBoer, who generally see the value in dissent and radical critiques of prevailing norms. Why is education different?

EIGHT

Some Evangelical Christian Homeschooling Limits the Worldly Options of Girls

Kathryn Joyce

Quiverfull is a movement among conservative evangelical Christians that shuns birth control completely. Quiverfull families are typically patriarchal, with clearly defined gender roles that place women under the authority of men. Quiverfull families also believe strongly in homeschooling. In the following viewpoint, an excerpt from her book titled *Quiverfull: Inside the Christian Patriarchy Movement*, journalist Kathryn Joyce describes the role and education of daughters in Quiverfull families. Because of the subservient role of women in this subculture, the education of girls focuses on homemaking. They are sheltered from the outside world, and college is not considered an option for them.

There were complications when Anna Sofia Botkin, the eldest daughter of Geoffrey Botkin, one of Vision Forum's leading voices and an elder-in-training for Doug Phillips's church, Boerne Christian Assembly, was born. Her mother, Victoria Botkin, might have died. While doctors attended to the post-labor mother,

Geoffrey Botkin held his newborn daughter perfectly still in his cupped hands, and prayed to God for guidance: after having raised two older sons, how should he raise a daughter? As he prayed, he felt God move him to a specific prayer for the infant sleeping in his hands, a prayer for her body. He remembered baby girls are born with two ovaries and a finite number of eggs that will last them a lifetime. He placed his hand over his new daughter's abdomen and prayed for Anna Sofia to be the "future mother of tens of millions." He prayed that the Lord would order everything in his daughter's life: "What You will do with every single egg here. How many children will this young lady have? Who will be her husband? With what other legacy will these little eggs be joined to produce the next generation for the glory of God?" He explained to a room full of about six hundred fathers and daughters gathered for the annual Vision Forum Father and Daughter Retreat that he had prayed that his new daughter might marry young.

Multigenerational Faithfulness

Today, Anna Sofia and her sister, Elizabeth, strikingly poised young women in their early twenties, are the preeminent Vision Forum brand for promoting biblical womanhood to the unmarried daughters of homeschooling families, girls largely raised in the patriarchal faith but susceptible to temptations from the outside world. In all their testimony to fellow young "maidens," the Botkin daughters, raised in both the American South and the Botkins' Seven Arrows Ranch in New Zealand, stress the dire importance of one of their father's favorite talking points: "multigenerational faithfulness." That is, the necessity of the sons and daughters of the movement—especially the daughters—cleaving to the ways of their parents and not abandoning the dominion project the older generation has begun. . . .

As Jennie Chancey tells the Botkin sisters in their book, *So Much More: The Remarkable Influence of Visionary Daughters on the Kingdom of God*, children of the movement should have "little to no association with peers outside of family and relatives" as insulation from a corrupting society. Daughters shouldn't forgo education but should consider to what ends their education is intended and should place their efforts in "advanced homemaking" skills.

Homemaking Is More Important than Education

Concretely, Geoffrey Botkin explains, this means evaluating all materials and media that daughters receive from childhood on as it pertains to their future role. The Botkin sisters received no Barbie dolls—idols that inspire girls to lead selfish lives—but rather a "doll estate" that could help them learn to manage a household of assets, furniture, and servants in the aristocratic vision of Quiverfull life which Botkin paints for the families around the room. The toys the girls played with were "tools for dominion," such as kitchen utensils and other "tools for their laboratory": the kitchen.

R.C. Sproul, Jr., in a book of advice to homeschooling parents, *When You Rise Up*, describes the critical secret of God's covenants as the cornerstone of the homeschool movement: the imperative of covenants, he says, is to "pass it on to the next generation." He's done so himself, he relates, in what he calls the R.C. Sproul, Jr., School for Spiritual Warfare, in which he crafts "covenant children" with an "agrarian approach" and stresses that obedience is the good life in and of itself, "not a set of rules designed to frustrate us but a series of directions designed to liberate us." In that freedom, boys and girls are educated according to their future roles in life, and girls are taught that they will pursue spiritual warfare by being keepers in the home.

To gauge the amount of secular baggage his homeschooling readers are trailing, he tells the story of a family friend whose homeschooled nine-year-old daughter still cannot read. "Does that make you uncomfortable?" he asks.

Are you thinking, "Mercy, what would the superintendent say if he knew? . . . But my friend went on to explain, "She doesn't know how to read, but every morning she gets up and gets ready for the day. Then she takes care of her three youngest siblings. She takes them to potty, she cleans and dresses them, makes their breakfasts, brushes their teeth, clears their dishes, and makes their beds." Now I saw her rightly, as an overachiever. If she didn't know how to read but did know all the Looney Tunes characters, that would be a problem. But here is a young girl being trained to be a keeper at home. Do I want her to read? Of course I do. . . . But this little girl was learning what God requires, to be a help in the family business, with a focus on tending the garden.

Young girls participate in a prayer circle at an evangelical school. Critics of such schools say that girl students are sheltered from the outside world and not presented with the option of going to college, only of becoming a homemaker.

Withdrawal from the World

It's this kind of separatist, radical thinking, advocating both physical and mental withdrawal from the world of public schooling, that informs the mission of E. Ray Moore, a retired Army chaplain and head of the homeschool ministry Exodus Mandate. Michael McVicar, who studies Reconstructionism and has written about [Christian theologian and homeschool movement pioneer] R.J. Rushdoony, sees Moore's homeschool ministry as one of the most direct embodiments of Rushdoonys ideas. Exodus Mandate, as its name hints, expresses an explicitly secessionist ethos that aims for ultimate removal of Christian families from state rule—leaving "Pharaoh's school system" for the Promised Land—but in the intermediate future, pushes Christians to remove their children from public schools as a ploy to collapse by attrition what they consider a wicked, humanist institution. . . .

Defying Culture

The patriarchy community, . . . is dedicated to building up its own, purist alternatives to the interaction mainstream society provides. Vision Forum gears its entire Beautiful Girlhood catalogue collection—replete with tea sets, white gloves, "modesty slips," and Victorian manners books—to the proper raising of daughters in the faith. Both Vision Forum and the Chalcedon Foundation sponsor girls' essay contests on subjects such as fulfilling one's vocation as a daughter and the enduring appeal of Elsie Dinsmore—a heroine in Martha Finley's Victorian-era children's book series, an obedient and priggishly pious daughter of the Antebellum South who aspired to be a submissive daughter and wife. (Dinsmore, as one contest winner wrote, shows daughters how "to rise up by stepping down.")

Elaborate courtship mechanisms are being worked out by fathers hoping to make alliances through the marriages of their daughters to the sons of men in the fold. And home business projects, largely home-based sewing businesses that produce modest clothing or home decorations, are cropping up among young daughters of the movement to such an extent that in 2007 James and Stacy

McDonald urged homeschooled daughters to consider signing up with a new young-woman's home business ministry, the Proverbs 31 Project. The project, evoking the many virtues of the storied Proverbs 31 woman, is a Mary Kay [cosmetics]–like franchise that promises to help young daughters "build a business for herself around the use of therapeutic-grade essential oils," thereby helping her find a way to bring a home business into her marriage, making her a more attractive prospect to potential suitors.

"There's a generation of daughters in this room today that we have not seen for one hundred years of American history," exclaimed one of the speakers at the Vision Forum Father and Daughter Retreat, Scott Brown. He attributes the rise of this new breed of daughters to a "revival in the land." But it's also the fruit of twenty-five years of work, he says, when parents turned their hearts to their children and began doing "many culture-defying things," such as homeschooling their children, fighting feminism, and leading their daughters in the opposite direction of women's lib. . . .

The Evils of Feminism

Model daughters of the patriarchy movement, the Botkin girls express a hatred of feminism that is pure, and they hate it in a variety of flavors most feminists wouldn't recognize as their cause. To the Botkins, all bad women—from the seductress hoping to "subdue masculinity" with her womanly wiles and charms to vain pageant queens to career women to even conservative Christian wives who aren't fervent enough about spiritual war—are feministic, seeking to "weaken and dominate men."

On stage, the sisters explained to an audience of fathers and daughters, young women to very young girls, the ways in which daughters should go beyond a lukewarm acceptance of biblical femininity to a full-on embrace of a deliberately countercultural girlhood. They should be modest servants who don't cause their brothers in Christ to stumble with temptation. They should "learn to ignore [their] comfort zone" in the interest of a higher calling, as Elizabeth, a formerly terminally shy child, describes her

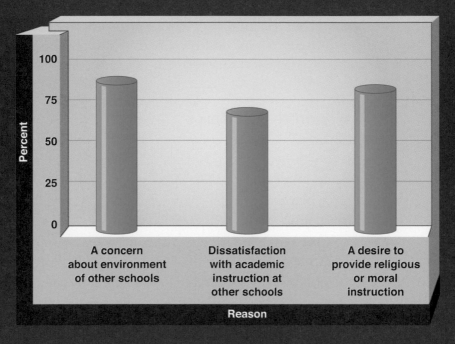

Most Parents Homeschool to Protect Their Children

Percent

100

75

50

25

0

| A concern about environment of other schools | Dissatisfaction with academic instruction at other schools | A desire to provide religious or moral instruction |

Reason

Taken from: US Department of Education, National Center for Education Statistics. Parent and Family Involvement in Education Survey of the 2007 National Household Education Surveys Program (NHES).

father's insistence on her "godly boldness." They should teach their younger sisters in the Titus 2 [referring to the second chapter of the New Testament Epistle to Titus] spirit and should honor and defer to their brothers—older and younger—in recognition that even young boys need to be treated as wise leaders by their older sisters in order to gain the confidence to be leaders of their future families. They should wear feminine clothes to prove to their fathers that they are virtuous women worthy of protection. They should not learn career skills as emergency "backups" to support themselves, as "learning to 'survive' can teach girls attitudes of independence, hardness." They should understand that singleness is a very rare calling from God, and so they must prepare to marry and conduct war on "the home front": in other words, they must understand there is no opting out of this revolution without turning their backs on the faith. But most of all, the Botkins explain, a virtuous daughter should "turn her heart to her father" in the spirit of Malachi 4:6: "And he shall turn the heart of the fathers to the children, and the heart of the children to their fathers, lest I come and smite the earth with a curse."

Submission to All Men

The turning of daughters' hearts to their fathers is the driving theme of the retreat, which besides the Botkin girls, features the sermons and messages of Doug Phillips, Geoffrey Botkin, and Scott Brown, a board member of Vision Forum and a leader in Phillips's family-integrated church movement. All three men explain what is at stake to the girls and young women in the room: they are daughters of Zion, of Judah, of Jerusalem. They are future mothers of Israel. As such, they have no time to waste, or spirits to risk, by leaving home for college, work, or missions. They must instead make the revolutionary choice to "redeem the years" they have with their fathers and view their single lives as preparation for marriage: submitting themselves to their fathers and, to some extent, their brothers, as they will one day submit themselves to their husbands.

NINE

Christian Homeschooling Should Not Limit the Options of Girls

Jeannette Webb

Some evangelical families that homeschool limit the education of their daughters, preparing them not for college, but to be wives and mothers. Jeannette Webb, a homeschooling mother and educational consultant (aiming higherconsultants.com), draws from personal experience in the following viewpoint. She argues that while homeschooling parents should raise their daughters to be submissive to their husbands and should include homemaking skills in their daughters' educations, they should also prepare their daughters for college and let them explore their academic interests. A good college education, says Webb, will make them stronger women and potentially allow them to earn enough income working part-time that they will be able to homeschool their own children.

Perhaps one of the most delicate issues facing the homeschool community today deals with our daughters. Just how exactly are we to raise, train, and educate them?

As parents, most of us are recovering from the devastation that postmodernism and feminism imposed on our younger lives. We have repented our youthful worldviews and gone running in the opposite direction. We don't want our daughters to make the same mistakes that we made or live with the disconnect that we felt.

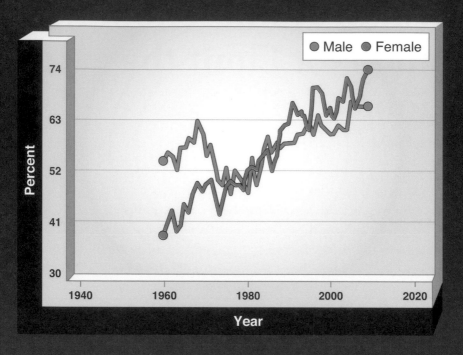

Percentage of Recent High School Completers Attending College: 1960 to 2009

Year

Percent

● Male ● Female

Taken from: US Census Bureau, Statistical Abstract of the United States: 2012.

If we were highly educated, perhaps we focus our home educating away from the academic side. If we dated freely throughout our teen years, perhaps we think our girls should not date at all and not even talk to males. If we rarely attended church, maybe we try to take our kids every time the church doors open.

No one could deny that our intentions are good and our motives are pure. History, however, teaches us that swinging to the opposite extreme is rarely the best course of action. Instead, we need a thoughtful response to a tough issue. This will require a great deal of prayer and the ability to move outside a popular homeschool box. Unfortunately, for a movement that was once so dynamic and original, shackles of guilt are being clamped around us by popular ministries and speakers.

Teaching Daughters to Be
Submissive but Also Strong

It goes without saying that our goal is to raise girls with a gentle and quiet spirit who understand the delicate balance of joyful submission to God and husband. However, I am afraid that we have too often equated submission with unthinking compliance. Somehow when I look at the strong women of the Bible, I think we've missed the point on this one. Scripture shows us multifaceted women with inner vitality, intelligence, leadership ability, and business acumen. This wasn't threatening to their men, rather their noble characters caused them to be praised in the gates (something uncommon in Israel).

While I would never presume to understand the mystery of submission, I have an idea that there is something infinitely more appealing when a capable and intelligent woman yields headship out of love and respect than a doormat who has nothing to give up and therefore nothing to offer. I love Randy Sims' definition of meekness in *The Greatest Among You*. He says that true meekness is "power under control." What a beautiful picture.

I loved the years I spent training my daughter in homemaking skills. She learned to cook, can, garden, bake bread, sew, crochet, clean house, and set a beautiful table—all before the age of 10. Then it was time to incorporate other things. As a young teen she worked by my side acquiring skill sets in time management, communications, business, leadership, and community development. I saw her time as more valuable than my own because I knew that I only had a few years for this on-the-job training.

We must remember that we are there for our children. Not the reverse. While many hands make light work, they were not given to us to do our job. If we make the decision to have a large family, we must continue to parent all the way to the end. It is not the job of a competent older daughter to raise our babies.

Allowing Children to Pursue
Their Educational Passions

While I would certainly never argue that college is for every girl, we need to push the envelope of what is possible for our daughters.

Set the expectation at college entrance requirements (four years of math, science, language arts, social studies, and foreign language). Then, if your student absolutely can go no further, stop without guilt. But, be advised that your students may be capable of much more than you give them credit for. Be aware too that your fear of certain subjects can transfer to them. If you think they can't do it, you will certainly convince them of that.

Let me give you an example. My son was a born scientist. From the age of two he adamantly refused nursery rhymes and fairy tales and demanded insect-identification books for bedtime stories. His vocabulary was light years ahead of his peers. He was fascinated with the physical world and spent his entire childhood reading vociferously on many science topics. I knew where he was headed without a doubt.

Then there was my daughter—a girl who loved the color pink, tea parties, and baby dolls. I had raised one scientist and she was nothing like him. By the age of 8 she was the undisputed pie-baking champion in our church of excellent cooks. By the age of 10 she kept our household running during a prolonged illness of mine. She was an accomplished musician and an endearing public speaker. A very capable student, she did not show the academic passion of her older brother; however, we required the same college prep high school program for both students. College was our expectation, but I honestly thought we were looking at a music or communications major (which was fine with me).

Then AP [advanced placement] Biology happened, and it was like watching a miracle unfold before my very eyes. At the age of 15, my little girly girl suddenly emerged as a force to be reckoned with. She poured herself into the rigorous class and surpassed her brother's scores. She leapt ahead in math and conducted genetics research at a local university. Today she is pursing an extremely rigorous engineering program at Princeton and loving every minute of the challenge.

My heart still flutters when I realize that I almost missed it. Had I not expected her best academically and pushed her to find it, she would never have discovered the fine mind that God gave her and a career field that she loves. It brought me to the harrowing realization that I do not have the wisdom to pre-determine my child's capabilities and calling. I do not have the right to limit her because of my limits. I dare not thwart her development because of my fear. It was truly one of the most sobering moments of my life.

A Carefully Planned Career Path Allows Women More Time with Family

As a professional woman, I had a very fulfilling career, but it was one that required horrible hours and did not pay well. Neither was there any possibility of part-time employment. I have to admit that there were a few years (when our diet consisted mainly of casseroles, oatmeal, lentils, and fruit from our orchard) that I would have welcomed the opportunity to help my husband with some part-time work.

Contrast that with a homeschooling friend of mine who is a pharmacist. She works a very flexible part-time schedule (usually a day or two over the weekend while her husband is at home with the kids) and makes more money than I made while working a 50-hour week and never seeing my family. She home educated her children, taught science and math classes for her co-op, coached the sports team, and had the security of knowing that she was helping the family finances without the family suffering for it.

The difference in our stories was that she carefully chose a career and paid the price early to secure her future. I followed a career path that was interesting, but I gave no thought as to the potential security it would provide for my family. My daughter has learned from my mistake.

Training Daughters to Have a Robust Life

I have yet to find scriptural support for the insidious conviction that the focus of a young woman's life is to find a husband. The way I read things, the goal of her life is to love God and love her neighbor. Her single years, whether they be few or whether they last a lifetime, are to be rich and fulfilling and glorifying to our Creator.

The author argues that while homeschooling parents should teach their daughters to be submissive to their husbands and to be homemakers, they should also prepare them for college and let them explore their academic interests.

We do our daughters a disservice if we encourage them to sit and wait for life to happen to them. I have watched this strange phenomenon for years and the results are rarely pretty. Rapunzel gets stuck in the tower, grows old, and becomes embittered.

Another too-common scenario is that Prince Charming springs her from her prison, but is unskilled and unable to provide well (after all, the princely virtues of writing poetry and sketching his true love's face don't transmute well into cash) or he doesn't live long enough to raise the large family and Rapunzel finds that her untrained vocal performances only bring in starvation wages.

As much as I would like to predict my daughter's future (loving husband, brood of healthy homeschooled children, beautiful home, and financial stability), I figured out some time back that I was not God. As much as I would dream and scheme and try to manipulate circumstances, I am honestly in control of nothing. My daughter's life is as fragile as the china tea cups she collects. To be fair to her, I must train her to live a robust life, ready for the joys and the heartbreaks that will inevitably be hers.

To do this, I must let go of the reins so she can find out who she is and what life holds for her. I must encourage her to sharpen her mind, to fully develop her gifts, and then, model for her how to trust God with the outcome. After all, He loves her more than I do.

TEN

Homeschooling Can Be a Feminist Act

Becky Ellis

With so much media attention on the conservative Christian side of homeschooling, self-proclaimed feminist mom Becky Ellis offers a different perspective. In this viewpoint, Ellis argues that homeschooling—or home-based education—supports feminism and is good for both boys and girls. She favors homeschooling because she feels it protects children from the public school environment that pressures children into gender stereotypes. In addition, homeschooling allows children to spend time with feminist parents who share both income and housekeeping responsibilities. Ellis makes the point that even girls from antifeminist homeschooling families are more resistant to gender-based stereotypes if they are encouraged to follow their own interests.

I am a feminist. In fact, most people who know me would say that feminism informs practically everything I do: what I read, how I relate to people, what forms of political action I undertake—everything, some might say, except my decision to home-school my children.

To many, this is one part of my life that seems out of line with my feminist politics. For one thing, friends have pointed out, it makes the structure of my family seem strangely traditional: my children's dad makes the money and I do more of the child care. And my decision to home-school means, in effect, that I will not be able to have a full-time career until my children are grown up.

Then there's the broader social context. The public image of the home-schooling mother most often portrayed in mainstream pop culture is that of a God-fearing woman who devotes her life to her husband, children and home. For example, a series of reality TV shows about the Duggar family—a home-schooling fundamentalist family with 17 children—ran recently on The Learning Channel and the Discovery Health Channel. The Duggars have appeared on many mainstream talk shows as well, including The View and Jimmy Kimmel Live. And this depiction isn't entirely divorced from reality: a U.S. study by the National Center for Education Statistics found that 72 per cent of home-schooling parents surveyed indicated that "providing religious or moral instruction" was one of their reasons for home-schooling. For 38 per cent, it was their main reason.

It is no secret that many home-schoolers in North America are strict evangelical Christians—a group that is staunchly opposed to feminism, to reproductive rights for women, and to civil rights for gays, lesbians, transgendered people and bisexuals. Not exactly the company I keep.

How Public Schools Hurt Boys

A recent article on the Fox News website goes as far as to posit home-schooling as a direct challenge to feminism: an opportunity for families to protect their children (particularly their boys) from the forces of feminism, which have, according to the author, created a "PC" [politically correct] education system that "shortchanges" boys.

Obviously, I don't see it that way. In fact, for me one of the most troubling features of today's public education system is the pervasiveness of sexism and sexual violence in schools. In fact, a recent report by the Toronto [Ontario, Canada] District School Board found that "violence against girls and young women is a pervasive problem" in Toronto public schools. Sexual harassment of girls by boys is too common; sexist attitudes and stereotypes continue to negatively affect the self-confidence and personal development of girls and boys; and the influence of peers, teachers and curriculum tend, in both overt and subtle ways, to pressure children into restrictive gendered boxes that distort the way they think, act, and try to look. So, yes, boys are harmed by what happens in schools today. But the problem is too little feminism,

The Duggar family is the stereotype of a homeschooled fundamentalist Christian family. The Duggars chose homeschooling in order to provide their children with religious and moral instruction.

not too much. In fact, if the public system were really pushing a feminist and queer-positive agenda as the Fox article alleges, my son would probably be sitting in a cold, hard desk seat right now.

Feminist Homeschoolers

I know I'm not alone. A vocal minority of home-schoolers are progressives, even radicals, who home-school as a way to offer their children the freedom to explore their intellectual interests and to express themselves in a loving, nurturing environment. Countless progressive home-schoolers (many of whom practice "unschooling," an unstructured, child-directed approach to learning) not only reject the conservative beliefs about women and families held by evangelical Christians, but are in fact creating new ways of arranging families and of living and learning in a feminist way.

For one thing, feminist home-schooling families are usually not as traditional in their structure as they might at first appear. In my own case, the imbalance in money making may look conventional, but all domestic duties—cooking, cleaning, laundry, and so on—are divided equally. And although I don't get paid for it, I am a full-time student completing my BA; I'm also a dedicated community activist. All the feminist home-schooling parents I talked to for this article were engaged in some sort of employment outside the home. This included one restaurant owner, a few writers, a chaplain at a hospital, two doulas [midwives], and one individual who makes and sells baby slings.

Family Structure

While it is true that the majority of home-schoolers are from two-parent households in which the father makes the most income, 18 per cent of home-schooling families in the U.S. are single-parent households. This means that these families are finding creative ways to home-school even when society makes it hard for them to be with their children for the majority of their time while surviving financially. Homeschooling outside of the traditional family unit can create new and alternative forms of family structure, which can further help to challenge sexism in our society.

As Adriana Johnson, a home-schooling mom of two from Calgary [Alberta, Canada], tells me, "We describe our financial situation as 'two people working three-quarters of a job between them for one income.' We are both self-employed and work from home. On average weeks, each of us spends the equivalent of two full-time workdays, maybe three, on paid work." The vision of a home-schooling family as one in which the mother is immersed in domestic duties does not reflect the lived experiences of many home-schooling feminist parents. In fact, choosing to home-school one's children is in many ways the opposite of choosing to work at domestic duties. Catharine Crawford, an unschooling mom of three from southwestern Ontario, explains: "Feminism lets me choose to be home-based in my own way, and celebrate all my strengths, be they culturally constructed as masculine or feminine. My work as a feminist is to counter the way in which culture has warped biological difference into an essentialist, inequitable framework for living as 'female' or 'male.'"

Many of the mothers I talked to emphasized the need to put value on the work they do as home-schooling parents as a way to counter the seemingly traditional arrangement of their families. Crawford explains to her children that, "Papa has gone to work, and it is my work to stay home with you."

Home-schooling encourages my children and I to explore our interests together—though when our interests diverge we don't hesitate to explore them separately. I knit, garden, do activist work, and engage in my intellectual pursuits alongside my children. With a few exceptions, home-schooling does not limit me in exploring my interests; only child-unfriendly barriers do.

Community-Based Learning

As a feminist and politically progressive home-schooler, I sometimes feel the tension of having rejected the publicly funded education system for what many regard as an individual solution to the current problems in the mainstream education system.

However, the term "*home*-schooling" actually fails to capture the breadth of my day-to-day life with my kids; we often spend much of the day out in nature or using public resources such as libraries and community centres. We regularly co-operate with other home-schoolers, attend community activities, and interact with our neighbours and other folks in our city. We spend much of our spring and summer, for example, at our community garden plot, working and learning alongside the other gardeners. It would be more accurate to think of what we do as community-based learning rather than home-schooling.

Freedom from Gender Stereotyping

Many of the home-schooling mothers I spoke to mentioned how a relaxed or "unschooling" approach to home-schooling allows their children to fully explore all their interests, free from the restrictions of gender stereotyping. Children are supported in learning in whatever ways come most naturally to them as individuals, regardless of their gender. As Johnson describes, "My daughter learns by listening and modelling. My son learns by experimenting and doing. I do not try to force her to learn the way he does, nor him the way she does—there is no artificial mould into which they have to fit." Nancy, a home-schooling mother of six from Toronto, also echoes the benefits of this approach in countering sexist attitudes in our society: "I try to keep my daughter aware of the things that she might like to do, like math and science (my favourites). My second son loves little figurines—he has a cabinet full of beautiful tiny things, because that's who he is. Nobody ever said that 'boys don't do that.'"

In fact, freedom from gender stereotyping is one of the benefits most mentioned by the feminist home-schoolers with whom I spoke. My feminism is informed by a queer perspective that gives me a decidedly anti-essentialist view of gender and sexuality. One of my main motivations to home-school is to allow my children to develop into full human beings without the restrictions of oppressive gender categorizations.

Johnson mentions some strategies that she and her partner consciously employ to foster gender-free development. "They are free to be themselves. Sometimes that means acting like 'typical' boys and girls. And sometimes that means something quite different or opposite or out of this world. Our son wore a princess dress to every party for about two years (also rubber boots and a military cap, with a water pistol, frequently as part of the costume too)."

She describes how she and her partner both participate in all household tasks—from baking to using power tools—and how she plays around with gender when reading books to her children, to ensure that they "know a variety of people filling a variety of roles."

Challenging Cultural Assumptions

The mothers I interviewed also mentioned challenging some of the ideas about gender their children encounter in broader society. As Catharine Crawford, the unschooler from southwestern Ontario, says,

> Being home-based with my children allows all of us to question cultural assumptions, and tease them out in a relaxed way. My children are free to behave and make choices with less influence from stereotypes of what it is to be male or what it is to be female. Schooled children are not always given the time to see the cages we have built for our gendered selves, but in our free-range living here, we can feel free to be girly or boyish if we choose to.

Linda Clement, an unschooling mother of two from Victoria, describes her home-schooling experience as allowing each of her children to be viewed as "a whole, complex, exploring human. If he wants to curl his hair, it's his hair. If she wants a buzz cut, it's her head. If she wants to read the big book of monster trucks, they're her eyeballs. If he wants to read the sappy melodrama, they're his eyes."

Home-schooling can give children the freedom to learn in a truly feminist way. In my classroom, women are never written

Learning advantages and family closeness were the most reported benefits of "unschooling".

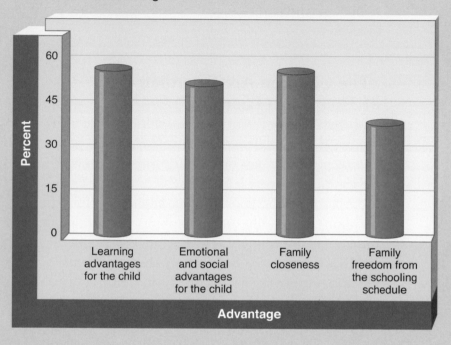

Taken from: Peter Gray. "The Benefits of Unschooling: Report I from a Large Survey." *Psychology Today,* February 28, 2012.

out of history. In fact, feminist history is part of what I discuss with my children. More than that, however, I teach them how to critically engage with the world: to question assumptions and biases (even those coming from me!) and to think about what might be missing from an historical account or who might have a different perspective than the one being presented. As Beatrice Ekwa Ekoko, who puts together a weekly radio show called Radio Free School with her children, remarks, "If you are encouraging your child's curiosity, inquisitiveness and questioning of all that they see, then I think you can raise some pretty tough-minded feminist children—female or male."

Of course, many teachers in the public system also share a feminist perspective—but others don't. Some teachers are anti-feminist and others don't question or challenge sexism in a very meaningful manner. Such is the reality of raising children in a society in which sexism still runs deep, in spite of advances on many fronts.

"The Children Are Guardians of Their Own Learning"

Although I reject essentialist descriptions of women as less competitive than men, I do think that feminists have tended to value a less competitive, less hierarchical approach to learning, particularly at the university level. Home-schooling, especially unschooling, takes a similar approach but applies it to children. There is no testing, no grading and no ranking. My children explore their intellectual interests because they want to, not because they have to. They are empowered to create their own learning path, with me as an active facilitator. Far from limiting my children, this approach has led them to explore a wide range of interests at a very young age.

As Crawford points out, "An anti-sexist learning approach means letting children unfold in a way unfettered by cultural assumptions because the children are guardians of their own learning. There is little pressure from grown-ups about what's 'appropriate' for one's age or gender. There is time to question, and time to be aware of ourselves and our choices. It is wonderful."

Confident Girls

The 1996 book *A Sense of Self: Listening to Home-schooled Adolescent Girls* by Susannah Sheffer explores the way in which home-schooling allows girls to become confident about their intellectual and physical capabilities and allows them to resist gender stereotyping by exploring their interests without being limited by gender roles. Sheffer, who interviewed 50 home schooled girls, found that even when their parents did not support feminism, the girls, in being encouraged to explore their own interests, grew to be relatively free of harmful gender stereotypes. Statistics about the academic achievements of home-schoolers consistently show that home-schooled children score above schooled children in standardized testing. A study by the National Home Education Research Institute showed that homechooled children outperformed schooled children on standardized tests by 30 to 37 per cent in all subjects. Similar statistics gathered by various state education departments in the United States have found similar results. Although as an unschooler I have serious objections to standardized testing being used as a measure of knowledge or ability, these statistics do seem to point to the positive results of individualized, child-led learning.

While home-schooling can create some challenges for a woman trying to live a feminist life, the home-schoolers I spoke to have all found that it can also be a deeply feminist act. As Beatrice Ekwa Ekoko says, "If feminists care about a good future for women, then looking at institutions that oppress and degrade women and children ought to extend into looking at the places where some of these have their beginnings: namely, the school." The common perception of home-schooling as conservative and closed-minded needs to challenged and replaced with a more complex view of home-schooling families, and with further exploration of what feminist pedagogy for children can look like. Feminist home-schooling can provide an important alternative to conventional ways of educating and socializing children—and of organizing families.

ELEVEN

The Health of a Family: Homeschooling from the Heart

Julie Foster

Faced with both the stress of being overbooked and the financial strain of private schooling, family nurse practitioner Julie Foster and her husband looked to homeschooling. In this viewpoint Foster explains how homeschooling transformed her family for the better. Her children were able to self-direct their educations and had time to explore their interests, including athletic endeavors, cultural projects, and a meaningful family genealogy project. Her high school daughter was able to prepare for college, spend extra time writing, and participate in extracurricular activities without feeling overbooked. Overall, the whole family was able to slow down and spend more time together.

Our family consists of a dad, a mom, two daughters, a son, a grandfather, a grandmother, four cats, one dog, two rabbits, and two bee hives—all of us living in the suburban rolling hills of Happy Valley, Oregon. The happiness and health of our family have been revealed through the many ways in which we've been striving and learning.

After having previously enrolled our children in a Waldorf school for nine years, we decided to homeschool our three children last year. We wondered what would be the best way for our children to learn, and we had to consider the rising costs of private education. But ultimately our decision seemed to be guided by a spiritual impetus.

About 13 years ago I had researched homeschooling when we lived rurally. My younger sister was the first to capture my attention for exploring another type of education as she chose to homeschool my niece and nephew for kindergarten and first grade. At the time, as a Family Nurse Practitioner, I had been exposed to homeschool families, and I was inspired and enchanted by the idea of being a central part of my children's education. As a mother and a professional, I often contemplated the quality time spent with my children.

Through my review of curriculum and pedagogical approaches, I stumbled across natural learning rhythms and a description of the three principal faculties of children; thinking, feeling, and willing (also known as head, heart, and hand) and began to see a way to educate the whole child. It resonated in me. A few years prior, through a series of coincidences, I had been introduced to and began my study of anthroposophic medicine. It wasn't until I moved back home to Portland, Oregon—pregnant with our third child and daunted by the thought of homeschooling—that I recalled how Waldorf education aimed to educate the whole child "from the inside out." It seemed to be the next best thing to homeschooling. (Not once did I feel public school was bad, but at the time I was intuitively drawn to something different.) We enrolled our eldest, then later our younger two children for the next nine years in a Waldorf school.

Neither my husband nor I attended private school as children, so we started the initial commitment of paying for private education without a long-term financial plan. At the time I was yet to set up my NP practice, and my husband (who was re-evaluating his professional career) was also diagnosed with cancer.

Even with financial assistance, I was driven to accept a second job—later, even a third—and my husband took on extra projects. In the back of my mind I remembered reading that the presence of the mother and the rhythm made in the home was essential, and that if the strain outweighed this then it defeated the goal of paying for a private education. Fortunately my children had the everyday blessing of grandparents for childcare, and we managed over the years to find the money almost like magic. We are firm believers in investing in something worthwhile, but as costs continued to increase, we had to reconsider our decision last year.

It was not just about finances. As a family, we generally felt overbooked and rushed. We wondered how it would be to simplify. The more we wanted to simplify, the more demanding life became. We loved our life, our jobs of service, and our community. But I had heard from homeschooling moms that time seemed to open up—that two and a half hours of homeschool time was equivalent to six hours of regular school.

How Homeschooling Works

So, after much consideration, we began homeschooling. The first few weeks were a real challenge. A friend had told me that it would be like we had moved to a foreign country, and absolutely I felt this. But throughout the process, I tried to think about and stay inspired by the success of a fellow medical colleague and her husband who have been homeschooling their seven children while maintaining their livelihoods and sanity.

My portion of our family's homeschooling plan is comprised of the main lesson (covering the main subjects required of each year), foreign language, and arts. For support, I use a Waldorf-based curriculum developed by Waldorf teachers Rainbow Rosenbloom and Bruce Bischof called Live Education! I study the curriculum for a week or two and prepare our calendar in advance so that on a day-to-day basis I can jump right in to the lessons. In the afternoons, my mother does handwork and my father teaches music. The children have had tutors to help with reading and writing. Physical education is integrated through team sports, horseback riding, dance, and swimming for this year. I am utilizing the public school for some electives and aim to continue the connection with our Waldorf school with plays, field trips, etc.

Homeschooling, the author argues, can help parents get closer to their children and allows more "quality time" for the family.

This last year while we were in Maui, my son trained for the Olympiad with a homemade javelin and discus, along with long jump, wrestling, and running lessons on the beach. Synchronicity would have it that the Haleakala Waldorf School had the Olympiad while we were in Maui and allowed him to participate. My daughter studied Tiki structures and constructed one while we were there for her third grade housing project. We visited a family farm and rode horses near the Haleakala Crater, saw a boar trap, and witnessed a baby goat being born. Meanwhile we also researched our family lineage and discovered gravesites that went back seven generations. These are just a few examples of how we made our homeschool time meaningful.

My high school student chose an online teacher-assisted program from Oak Meadow, an accredited college prep school out of Vermont, which allowed for moderate amount of parent involvement overseeing assignments. She took the opportunity to hone in on her writing and studying skills. She enjoyed setting her own pace and directing her schedule. Additionally she joined our district public high school equestrian team and took art and study skills classes. We are always seeking artistic endeavors, as I believe this is essential for the betterment of humanity.

We don't worry about lack of socialization since we are involved with our local community through various activities like sports and spiritual endeavors. We're also fortunate that our children have established friends and we can continue to foster the relationships. Plus there are many co-ops where other homeschoolers can take a class or share events. We remain focused on how to avoid overbooking ourselves as a family.

The entire homeschooling process has resulted in an intense transformation for our family. It's not without worry or frustrations. I let go of attempting to reproduce every aspect of what a public, private, or Waldorf school might offer and traded it for the intimacy and luxury of tailoring the day to what is essential for my children. The inner life I hold as a teacher sets the tone of each day. I find I must be prepared and then be flexible to let the children's needs at the moment guide the way. I knew we could not know the implications or insights of this choice until we entered into the experience, and the process continues to be astounding.

Feedback from our children displays the effects of our choice. My high school student says she loves homeschooling and doesn't miss the drama of her classmates, even though she has fond memories of her past experiences. Our younger two are content, and have expressed that they enjoy being home. One has even said, "I like that my mom takes the extra time with me when things are harder and we move faster when it's easy."

The experience is much richer than I could have imagined. Interestingly, time has indeed opened up. When I go to work I think, "Wow, today I've already spent quality time with my children." If homeschooling or work at my clinic become too demanding, I do feel a bit strained, so I constantly check in with myself through meditation, exercise, and spiritual self care. We aim to have family circles each Sunday to center each week. It is like a ritual to create a check in, set our intentions, and make a prayer. This gives all of us a frame of reference for how each of us is coping and invites the higher beings to guide and help us.

As a family we have slowed down and are enjoying so many things together. We save gas money from less running around and also plan meals and groceries more efficiently.

We had planned to homeschool for just one year, but we continue to analyze our decision from many angles. We know that there are many days and teachers being cut from public schools for budget concerns, and that we can save energy and time by not commuting. The aliveness we see in our children is fascinating and encouraging. So, at their insistence, we find that we are once again heading into a second year at home for our two youngest children. My high school student believes the concentrated time at home helped her develop better strategies for her dyslexia. Feeling more confident than before, she now has chosen to attend the public high school.

We will continue to take one day at a time to see what unfolds. There is so much more to share about the intricacies of our experience. I hope what we have shared inspires self-reflection for other families.

There are many ways to educate a child. As time goes by, we'll keep looking inside ourselves to take inventory. I think the homeschool experience has solidly grounded our children. Trying to determine the best way to educate our children in these times is a task we all share, and the health of society is paramount. As each of us discovers our life path and soul work, we contribute to the greater good. Through homeschooling, we have regenerated our family's life forces—which, to me, is priceless.

What You Should Know About Homeschooling

Reasons Parents Choose to Homeschool

In a study by the National Center for Educational Statistics (NCES), when parents were asked why they homeschooled, the top three reasons were:

- concern about the school environment (safety, drugs, negative peer pressure): 85 percent
- to provide religious or moral instruction: 72 percent
- dissatisfaction with academic instruction at other schools: 65 percent

When parents were asked what the *single most important* reason for homeschooling was, they answered:

- concern about the environment in other schools: 31 percent
- to provide religious or moral instruction: 30 percent
- dissatisfaction with academic instruction at other schools: 16 percent
- other reasons: 9 percent
- child has a physical or mental health problem: 7 percent
- child has other special needs: 7 percent

Approaches to Homeschooling

Just as no two schools are completely alike, no two homeschools are alike, but most homeschools fit into at least one of these homeschooling models:

- Structured learning: Similar to traditional school, but at home and directed by a parent. Instruction may be with a teacher/parent, a directed independent study, an online program or a combination of these. Usually a curriculum and plan are involved. One or many different educational philosophies may be employed.
- "Unschooling" or natural learning: Unstructured learning based on a child's interests. There are no monthly or semester plans, no workbooks, and no tests. Parents still supervise their unschooled students, looking for teachable moments, helping them find books and other materials of interest, or planning activities or trips where students can learn about their interests.
- Eclectic homeschooling: A combination of structured and unstructured learning.
- Hybrid homeschooling: A combination of some type of homeschooling and public or private education.

Homeschooling Is Difficult to Assess

Much research has been conducted and many statistics and reports have been released concerning homeschooling over the last decades by the US government, education groups, and homeschooling advocacy groups. The research findings from these varying entities are not always consistent with each other. Reasons include but are not limited to the following:

- The very nature of homeschooling makes information gathering difficult; the number of children attending public school is much easier to measure than the number of children who do not attend any school, but are homeschooled instead.
- Some advocacy groups are more in touch with specialized groups, resulting in research findings that reflect those groups more than others. The largest homeschooling advocacy groups are Christian.

Homeschooling Continues to Grow

Over the last several decades homeschooling has become increasingly popular in the United States. According to the

National Center for Educational Statistics (NCES), estimated numbers are:

- 1999: 850,000
- 2003: 1.1 million
- 2007: 1.5 million

Homeschooling advocacy groups estimate even higher numbers of homeschoolers. According to the National Home Education Research Institute, homeschooling is growing more rapidly than any other kind of education. Its estimates of the number of US homeschoolers include:

- 2003: 1.4 million
- 2007: 1.9 million

The Average Homeschooler

According to statistics in an NCES report, in 2007 the typical homeschooler looked like this:

- female
- white
- two parents
- two or more siblings
- one parent working
- at least one parent with a bachelor's degree
- annual family household income between $50,000 and $75,000
- living in a rural community

Disparities in Homeschooling

Racial Disparity. Overall, the numbers of homeschoolers are growing but not in every demographic. For example, between 2003 and 2007, according to the NCES, the numbers of African American homeschoolers decreased. According to the NCES, in 2007, the estimated percentage of students being homeschooled in each of the following groups were:

- White: 77 percent
- Black: 0.8 percent
- Hispanic: 1.5 percent
- Other: 3.4 percent

Income Disparity. Homeschooling is most common in two-parent households, households with one of two parents working, and in middle-income households. The percentage of students in each group that were homeschooled in 2007 were:

- Two parents: 3.6 percent
- One parent: 1.0 percent
- Living with two parents, one in workforce: 2.0 percent
- Living with two parents, both in workforce: 7.5 percent
- Living with one parent, in workforce: 1.3 percent
- Living with one parent, not in workforce: 1.5 percent
- Family income of $25,000 or less: 5.19 percent
- Family income of $25,001 to $50,000: 24.1 percent
- Family income of $50,001 to 75,000: 26.8 percent
- Family income of $75,000 or more: 33.2 percent

What You Should Do About Homeschooling

While homeschooling has become more mainstream and more accepted, it is still a controversial and sometimes emotional issue for many people. Homeschooled children and their parents may feel disconnected from the larger community of traditionally schooled children. Children in traditional schools might have preconceived ideas about homeschoolers.

Even if you do not have a personal connection to homeschooling, there are almost certainly homeschoolers in your community. Understanding homeschooling, getting involved with homeschooling issues, and reaching out to those who are homeschooled (or to traditional students if you are homeschooled) are good first steps.

Understand Homeschooling

By picking up this book, you have already demonstrated that homeschooling is something that you want to understand. The articles in this book cover a wide range of issues concerning homeschooling, but they by no means cover everything. The additional articles, books, websites, and organizations to contact that are in the appendixes offer good sources of information. Your local public or school librarian can help you acquire them as well as additional and perhaps more current information. When you read new information, keep an open mind, and try to understand all sides of the issues; look for homeschooling issues about which you feel passionate and for ways to get involved.

Reading about and discussing homeschooling is one way to better understand it, but remember you are reading someone else's opinion. A better way to understand something is through first-hand experience. Reaching out to homeschooled students is the next step in increasing your understanding.

Reach Out

Make a point to get to know students who are educated in a different way—in your neighborhood, at soccer practice, at religious institutions, or maybe even at your next family gathering. Ask them positive questions such as What do you like about homeschooling (or your school)? They probably will not mind talking about it, but you do not have to interview them, quiz them, or pump them for information. If you just spend time with them, you will build greater understanding—you will understand more about each other.

Increasing understanding is not the only reason to reach out to homeschoolers. While many homeschoolers are involved in numerous extracurricular activities, some are not. Encourage them to become involved in community sports and activities or your school's sports teams, political groups, and drama and music groups, if your district allows homeschoolers to participate. Additionally, most students can use more study partners. Study for college entrance exams together, do homework together. You can also learn about each other's ways of studying and learning.

Get Involved

Whether you are a homeschooler or not, you can become involved in issues pertaining to homeschooling. One timely topic is whether homeschooled students have the right to participate in sports and other extracurricular activities at the local public schools. Read up on the controversy, and find out what your school's policies are. If you disagree with them, write to school board members and principals, attend school board meetings, or find other ways to become involved in the discussion.

ORGANIZATIONS TO CONTACT

The editors have compiled the following list of organizations concerned with the issues debated in this book. The descriptions are derived from materials provided by the organizations. All have publications or information available for interested readers. The list was compiled on the date of publication of the present volume; names, addresses, phone and fax numbers, and e-mail and Internet addresses may change. Be aware that many organizations take several weeks or longer to respond to inquiries, so allow as much time as possible.

Alliance for Excellent Education
1201 Connecticut Ave. NW, Ste. 901
Washington, DC 20036
(202) 828-0828
fax: (202) 828-0821
website: www.all4ed.org

The Alliance for Excellent Education is a national policy and advocacy organization that works to improve national and federal policy so that all students can achieve at high academic levels and graduate from high school ready for success in college, work, and citizenship in the twenty-first century. To encourage public awareness and actions that support effective secondary school reform, the alliance publishes many briefs, reports, and fact sheets and publishes a biweekly newsletter, *Straight A's*, which provides information on public education policy and progress in an accessible format.

Alliance for School Choice
1660 L St. NW, Ste.1000
Washington, DC 20036
(202) 280-1990
fax: (202) 280-1989

e-mail: www.allianceforschoolchoice.org/contact
website: www.allianceforschoolchoice.org

The Alliance for School Choice is the nation's vanguard organization for promoting, implementing, and enhancing kindergarten through grade twelve (K-12) educational choice. In collaboration with a host of national and state allies, the organization seeks to create opportunities for systemic and sustainable educational reform that puts parents in charge.

American Homeschool Association (AHA)
www.americanhomeschoolassociation.org

The AHA is an organization created to network homeschoolers on a national level. Current AHA services include an online news and discussion list that provides news, information, and resources for homeschooling families.

The Heritage Foundation
214 Massachusetts Ave. NE
Washington DC 20002
(202) 546-4400
fax: (202) 546-8328
e-mail: info@heritage.org
website: www.heritage.org

The Heritage Foundation is a conservative public policy organization dedicated to promoting policies based on the principles of free enterprise, limited government, individual freedom, traditional American values, and a strong national defense. The Heritage Foundation believes that good governance on the state, not the federal, level and giving parents the power to choose the right method of educating their children—including homeschooling—are the best ways to improve education in the United States. The foundation's website provides articles on these and other issues.

Home School Legal Defense Association (HSLDA)
PO Box 3000
Purcellville, VA 20134

(540) 338-5600
fax: (540) 338-2733
e-mail: https://secure.hslda.org/hslda/feedback.asp
website: www.hslda.org

The HSLDA is committed to protecting the rights of parents to direct the education of their children. It provides legal assistance to homeschooling families challenged by state government or local school boards. HSLDA publishes the *Home School Court Report* quarterly newsletter and brochures about home education.

National Center for Education Statistics (NCES)
US Department of Education
Lyndon Baines Johnson Dept. of Education Bldg.
400 Maryland Ave. SW
Washington, DC 20202
e-mail: http://nces.ed.gov/help/webmail
website: http://nces.ed.gov

NCES is part of the US Department of Education and serves as the primary federal entity for collecting and analyzing data related to education in the United States and other countries. The center organizes training seminars, holds conferences, and publishes its findings in reports and in its publications, including the *Education Statistics Quarterly* and the *Digest of Educational Statistics*.

National Education Association (NEA)
1201 Sixteenth St. NW
Washington, DC 20036-3290
(202) 833-4000
fax: (202) 822-7974
e-mail: www.nea.org/home/827.htm

The NEA is a volunteer organization whose goal is to advance the cause of public education. The association lobbies legislators for school resources, campaigns for higher standards for the teaching profession, and files legal actions to protect academic freedom. At the local level, the association conducts professional workshops and negotiates contracts for school district employees.

The National Home Education Network (NHEN)

1779 Wells Branch Pkwy., Ste. 110 B #113
Austin, TX 78728
e-mail: info@nhen.org
website: www.nhen.org

The NHEN facilitates grassroots work for state and local home-schooling groups and individuals by providing information, net-working services, and public relations on a national level. The network tracks developments in legislatures, courts, and state boards of education and helps homeschooling families set up their own legis-lative watch committees. NHEN publishes the *NHENotes* monthly newsletter, the *NHEN Advocacy Report*, and the *In the News Report*, which tracks print media reports about homeschooling.

National Home Education Research Institute (NHERI)

PO Box 13939
Salem OR 97309
(503) 364-1490
fax: (503) 364-2827
e-mail: mail@nheri.org
website: www.nheri.org

The NHERI is a nonprofit research organization that collects, tracks, and analyzes research on home-based education. It seeks to educate the public about homeschooling research through speak-ing engagements and through its publication of the *Home School Researcher*.

National School Boards Association (NSBA)

1680 Duke St.
Alexandria, VA 22314
(703) 838-6722
fax: (703) 683-7590
e-mail: info@nsba.org
website: www.nsba.org

The NSBA serves the national needs of local school boards. The association seeks to raise awareness of school board issues, assists school boards and educators in the uses of technology, reports the results of research on education issues, and lobbies Congress. The NSBA publishes the monthly magazine *American School Board Journal* and the *School Board News*, a semimonthly newspaper.

US Department of Education
Lyndon Baines Johnson Dept. of Education Bldg.
400 Maryland Ave. SW
Washington, DC 20202
e-mail: www2.ed.gov/about/contacts/gen/index.html
website: www.ed.gov

The purpose of the US Department of Education is to ensure equal access to education and to promote educational excellence. The department provides grants to primary, secondary, and postsecondary educational institutions; offers financial aid to students for postsecondary education; and underwrites education research. It produces hundreds of publications annually, including *Community Update*, which informs readers about available resources, services, and publications.

BIBLIOGRAPHY

David H. Albert and Joyce Reed, *What Really Matters*. Toronto, ON: Alternate, 2010.

Laura Fairchild Brodie, *One Good Year: A Mother and Daughter's Educational Adventure*. New York: HarperPerennial, 2011.

Quinn Cummings, *The Year of Learning Dangerously: Adventures in Homeschooling*. New York: Perigee, 2012.

Jeannie A. Gudith, *The New Face of Education: How Homeschooling Goes from Counterculture to Mainstream*. Bloomington, IN: Balboa, 2012.

Sonya A. Haskins, *Homeschooling for the Rest of Us: How Your One-of-a-Kind Family Can Make Homeschooling and Real Life Work*. Minneapolis: Bethany House, 2010.

Robert Kunzman, *Write These Laws on Your Children: Inside the World of Conservative Christian Homeschooling*. Boston: Beacon, 2009.

Sherri Lisenbach, *The Everything Homeschooling Book: All You Need to Create the Best Curriculum and Learning Environment for Your Child*. Avon, MA: Adams Media, 2010.

Jennifer Lois, *Home Is Where the School Is: The Logic of Homeschooling and the Emotional Labor of Mothering*. New York: New York University Press, 2012.

Hillary McFarland and Megan Lindsay, *Quivering Daughters: Hope and Healing for the Daughters of Patriarchy*. Austin: DarkLight, 2010.

Gail Nagasako, *Homeschooling: Why and How*. Minneapolis: Two Harbors, 2011.

Mitchell L. Stevens, *Kingdom of Children: Culture and Controversy in the Homeschooling Movement*. Princeton, NJ: Princeton University Press, 2001.

Tammy Takahashi, *Zenschooling: Living a Fabulous & Fulfilling Life Without School*. Los Angeles: Hunt, 2010.

Peg Tyre, *The Good School: How Smart Parents Get Their Kids the Education They Deserve*. New York: Henry Holt, 2011.

Laura Grace Weldon, *Free Range Learning: How Homeschooling Changes Everything*. Prescott, AZ: HOHM, 2010.

Periodicals and Internet Sources

Rochelle Eisenberg, "Class Half-Full," *Baltimore Jewish Times*, February 2, 2007.

Amanda Gefter, "Preach Your Children Well," *New Scientist*, November 11, 2006.

Margaret Heidenry, "My Parents Were Educational Anarchists," *New York Times Magazine*, November 13, 2011.

Shirley Henderson, "Ending School Daze: Home-Schooling Is a Parent's Legal Right, but Is It the Right Choice for Your Child?," *Ebony*, September 2008.

Meredith Hines-Dochterman, "Home School: Some Districts Assist Families," *Cedar Rapids (IA) Gazette*, March 7, 2010.

Rod Liddle, "Who Is Right About Homeschooling? My Colleague James—or Everyone Else?," *Spectator*, September 23, 2006.

Priscilla Martinez, "Does It Work?," *Islamic Horizons*, January/February 2009.

Priscilla Martinez, "School Is Where the Home Is," *Islamic Horizons*, January/February 2009.

Lawana McGuffey, "Why We Homeschool," *Countryside & Small Stock Journal*, January / February 2011.

Douglas Monk, "Beware of Burnout: 'Dual Enrollment' Is Also an Option," *Countryside & Small Stock Journal*, January/February 2011.

National Center for Educational Statistics, "1.5 Million Homeschooled Students in the United States in 2007," *Issue Brief*, December 2008.

Linda Perlstein, "Do-It-All-(Yourself) Parents," *Newsweek*, February 6, 2012.

Duke Pesta, "Moral Relativism and the Crisis of Contemporary Education," *New American*, December 5, 2011.

Mariette Ulrich, "Why I Homeschool (Because People Keep Asking)," *Catholic Insight*, January 2008.

Timothy Brandon Waddell, "Bringing It All Back Home: Establishing a Coherent Constitutional Framework for the Re-Regulation of Homeschooling," *Vanderbilt Law Review*, vol. 63, no. 2.

Laura Grace Weldon, "Your Homeschooled Teen: Coming to Selfhood Through Work and Interests," *LILIPOH*, Winter 2012.

Robin L. West, "The Harms of Homeschooling," *Philosophy & Public Policy Quarterly*, Summer/Fall 2009.

INDEX

PICTURE CREDITS